THE DRAGON NEEDS WINGS

Reinventing Idealism

Aryan Dixit

ISBN 979-8-88805-341-6

To you

Contents

Author's Note

Hi! If you're just browsing through this book or if you've already bought it, welcome to the world of Idealism! My name is Aryan Dixit. That name rings no bells, I suppose. I am a (as of now) 17-year-old student residing in Bangalore, India. The first thought to strike you was probably my age. Perhaps you question whether a 17-year-old can really write about such a complex issue as a replacement to democracy. But what difference does this age make, in the era of the Internet. Yes, previously we had to live through years of democracy to gain experience with the matter. Today? With the Internet we can get the experiences of a million people at once! So do not judge my book through the coloured lenses of age (that benefits no one).

Regardless, I hope that this book invites you to a new line of thought. The matter of this book is far from its end goal. In fact, there is so much to uncover and unpack from what is written in every chapter. True to my word of originality, I have ensured that every single chapter discusses a new idea. I have noted that many books today have the unfortunate habit of ruminating over and over. Obviously, I've tried to ensure that this book is different. We won't discuss your life's problems and how a simple yet elegant solution is its panacea (trust me, there is no such healer).

This book is about hope: it's about how ideas can truly change the world. That's cliché, I can hear you say it. However, I am not discussing how every idea is possible. Nor do I claim to advertise a fool-proof solution to world problems. My book is about how to save the world. For every problem in this world, we have but one cure: the people. Without the ingenuity of people, there is no modern man. So, the essence of this book lies in the understanding of its base concept – Idealism. I hope this book gives you the same pleasure it gave me in writing it.

Let the dragons grow wings.

Introduction

'If you want to conquer the world, you best have dragons'
– George R R Martin

Dragons without wings are just fire-breathing lizards. A pretty sizeable speckled egg hatches in the grassy fields just off civilisation. From it emerges, well, you. You're a scaly, tiny four-legged creature who can breathe fire. But, of course, this situation is somewhat strange for you - you've never been a peculiar fire-mouthed animal. Then, suddenly, you notice large, towering giants around. Things are getting weirder: they're the problems you face personified. You can see the economy, politics and even your college degree standing around you, smirking. You try to speak out, breathing fire, but there's no point trying to burn their shoes - it doesn't hurt them. So instead, their boots try to stamp on your throat. You have one hope - to fly. But how do you fly if you don't have wings? There is a way - maybe more than one. This book is about one of them - Idealism. Yes, this book will give you wings (or so we hope)! The question now is: what is Idealism?

Idealism

Over the years, we have called Idealism many names. We knew it as the philosophy of mind and reality; or the unrealistic belief in perfection. This time it's different. Here, I refer to Idealism as I define it - a new concept.

We can define Idealism in many ways. But at its core, it consists of three major points:

1. The survival of the fittest: if you don't change, the world will change you.
2. Real change needs you to believe that the impossible is possible.
3. A constant cycle of change demands many Idealists.

This book addresses these values and how to achieve them. But why do you need to care?

Sprouting Wings

As the leathery boots of these giants begin to fall on you, you passionately discuss your hatred for the economic system. Fiery words, but you remain frozen under the foot. Then, suddenly, you feel a pair of supple wings grow out of your back. You arch them and swoop out just in time. But, unfortunately, your fellow dragons (lizards) don't make it.

We have all had that one moment where we realised that a problem was too big to solve. When I was 12-years-old, my mother took me to a nearby government school. Underfunded and overpopulated, many of the students were not able to retain concepts (it wasn't entirely the fault of the teachers: who had to teach 3-4 grades at once due to the small size of the school). Now, my mother operated her own NGO for empowering and educating the underprivileged – Tejomay Charitable Trust. I decided that I had to help: but I could not see how far my help would go anyway. Teaching someone two years older than I was about the basics of English, I began to understand the gravity of this issue. I remembered watching TV debates on the state of public schools in India: but what was the point of talking without action? We had to grow wings. But wings for one person were not enough: we needed to give everyone wings. Soon, quite a few people were involved in teaching (thanks, mainly, to the efforts of my mother) the underprivileged.

I wish I could say that it was a success; that public schools in India are now of pristine quality. But they aren't. Still, even the success of one girl in learning is a breakthrough worth cherishing. Perhaps when a few of us grew wings, the rest will find inspiration. After all, it was in a community of dragons that the giants fell.

The world has always had problems - many of which threaten us directly. However, we see a trend when we analyse how we beat each issue that came at us. Each one began with a small idea from a person who wanted a world radically different from theirs. They then gather a small following. Finally, one day, they get noticed, and soon people throng to them and change the world. Naturally, the time it takes varies greatly from a few days to a few centuries. Yet, in the end, the world is always better when you try to implement your thoughts. You're probably thinking about Nazis or such, arguing that I'm wrong. I will explain more in the first chapter.

The Mythical Island of Dragons

So that settles one part of the book. But why do you need to care about ideas like Webocracy, Unisism and Parsamanity? For you are only one while your problems are many.

You are courageous as a dragon: you grow wings and attack the giants. Initially, they ignore you. But you persist with your fiery onslaughts, hovering about them. You look back to your roots - there is no help coming. Your friends and supporters are just fire-breathing lizards. Finally, you realise that your attempts are futile. A giant fist grabs your neck, strangling you in its grasp.

Without an active community, efforts to change the world are useless. Unless you empower your fellow people, nothing can help them grow wings. But how do we garner such a society? Through Idealism. More specifically, by creating a community where work does not mean survival, where we find representation in totality. Idealism opens the gates to the mythical island of dragons.

Concluding the Introduction

The Dragon needs wings - and it's time they earned them. So, let's begin by showing you how to grow your wings. Idealism begins with the self, so why not start there.

Away we fly.

PART I

The dragon crawled from under the broken, white eggshell that was once his comfort zone - their home. They looked to the skies and the lands beyond. There was light and then there was more darkness. After all, what else was there in the world? They could breathe fire, but where were their wings? Alas, the tiny dragon had none. Perhaps they serve no real purpose, thought the child. How wrong they were. Soon, they came to learn of the nefarious giants who routinely trampled his kind. All the dragons would protest, but what good is shooting fireballs at the shoes of a giant? What is the point of a dragon without wings?

Idealism

Or, How to Change the Impossible
'Only the impossible is worth doing.'

– Akong Rinpoche

Human history is the tale of a few people told from the lenses of the many they impacted. But that was not always the case (Or maybe it was, people just didn't have the ability to write back then). If we were to look at history as a whole, perhaps the most noteworthy human was the child of a great ape mother, sibling to the mother of all chimpanzees. In their own time, they were utterly clueless that their sexual behaviour would impact their entire planet for many millenniums and by no means intended to. That was 6-7 million years ago. 340,000 years ago, lived the shared father of all humans. At the same time, our common mother enjoyed existence about 100,000 years later. However, these humans lived and died completely monotone lives throughout this time (I mean they saw a lot more action in their lives than many of us do, but in terms of conscious generational impact, nothing). But, then again, their very existence was an act of defiance, akin to flipping off the whole planet, or even universe, which tried to kill it (The Universe is constantly trying to end life with the millions of risks it possesses. If life existed elsewhere before, they were incredibly lucky, just as we are today as well). No matter how little we think we are doing, we're essential in the long run. We've always been a defiant species like that - no wonder we survived!

Yet no particular person stands out with prominence, despite our ancestors' altogether revolutionary choices. Why? Because no single person was prodigious enough to make these decisions - they were minor changes which compounded over generations. Nobody was ordering his fellow humans to become farmers miraculously. To believe that a solitary genius in a hunter-gatherer tribe decided to create a whole new way of living/farming is absurd. But that's what we do intrinsically (don't tell me you're different if you've only studied high school history)! This notion seems quite alluring and plausible from an entirely history-ignorant modern perspective. Such a mentality is ingrained in us primarily because of the way prehistory is often written about - as if humans were developing at unprecedented speeds. They were not. At least not as fast as you think. In (stark) contrast, modern humans are developing at this pace. So why have humans grown more in the last 50 years than in the 200 before that? Why have humans developed more in the previous 300 years than the millennium before? Why have humans grown more in the last few millennia than millions of years back? What is the reason? The growth of **Idealism**.

What is Idealism?

The philosophers amongst you might point out that there's already a philosophical conjecture titled Idealism. But, no. We aren't talking about that. To all of us today, Idealism means a person who strives for something unrealistic (or so we think). They don't shut up and sit at home, doing nothing about the problems they see. They're different from everyone else - they're dragons in a land of lizards. This book is about why you should be one of them. This book discusses my original philosophy, Idealism, taken in the simplest sense of the word. But first, let's get what an idealist is out of the way.

Idealism is not a political ideology (not precisely, at least). Idealism consists of the mindset, the socio-economic system, and political administration. In this chapter, Idealism is a methodology or attitude. Politician or terrorist, ideology does not restrain Idealism. From the Hindutva-led 'Akhand Bharat' idealists' (They believe in an Indian nation united with its subcontinent) to the wealth inequality campaign-led 'Occupy Wall Street' idealists (Their massive protests resonated with the idea of demanding equality for the 99%), all of them are idealists. The colloquial usage of the term transcends even politics and its related fields, even when talking about mere possibilities of an event taking place. Put in context, Idealism is the ritual which grants a dragon its wings.

There are always idealists on either side of the spectrum at any time. Donald Trump, conservative favourite and ex-US president, and Abu Bakr al-Baghdadi, ISIS leader, happened to be idealists simultaneously. Alternatively, take Narendra Modi, current Indian Prime Minister, and Basavaraj, Indian Naxalite General-Secretary. Idealism need not be religious/political (although it is most heated

Economic Growth Throughout History (GDP)

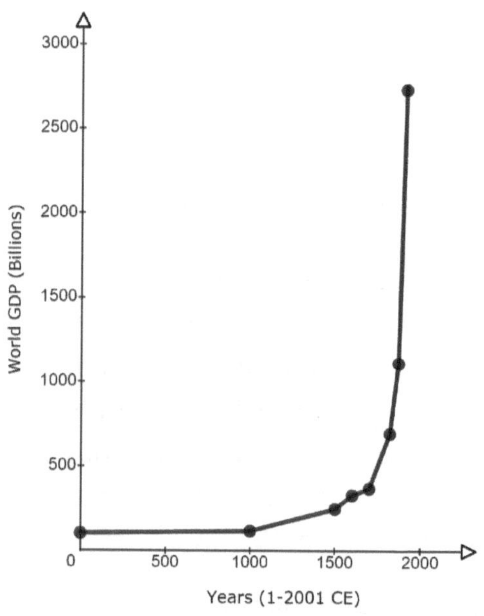

Economic growth worldwide has had a monumental increase over the past two centuries. This is matched by the rise in Idealism.

Source: The Maddison Project, University of Groningen Growth and Development Centre

there). For example, in science, the arguments of Francis Collins (author of *The Language of God*) against Richard Dawkins (author of *The God Delusion*) on the matter of theism. Or in music, with Sia's creative usage of Auto-tune, as opposed to Ed Sheeran's outright refusal. Idealism touches all spheres of life.

So, who exactly is an idealist?

1. A person (my deepest condolences to nonpersons reading this book)
2. Who believes in the popularly thought unrealistic
3. Strives to bring this change forth
4. Be it retrospectively good or bad for society
5. Be it successful or not

Shut Up and Save the World

All of these 'maxims' are integral to being an idealist and, thus, integral to society. However, while many of us can achieve points one and two (I sincerely hope), the onward postulates are far more challenging to achieve. Many of us have wishful ambitions to become our nation's president/PM/monarch, change half the laws, or inspire an intellectual revolution. Still, only a handful of us seems to be able to accomplish these goals—that handful of idealists who change the world. Why? We all talk about what we wish to change and seldom do it (ourselves). We sit around like fire-breathing lizards, aiming at the shoes of the giants. Everyone knows that this solves no problems - yet we continue our waste of flame. What we need to do is shut up and save the world.

Everyone can talk: and everyone does. But, because everyone can speak, no one gets heard. Through the smoke, even the brightest of flames dim. To be heard, you must act. And that's the difference between an optimist and an idealist. While idealists wish to see the world change and work on that desire, optimists believe that the world will change (inevitably) for the better. (Optimist: 'Humanity will change for the better.' Idealist: 'I will (try to) change humanity for the better.')

You Don't Need Success

Let's start from the final point: "Be it successful or not". The success of an idealist's venture is irrelevant to us calling them idealists. So, that has considerably broadened the ambit of people and historical figures who can be called idealists (Examples: Zeyd Ag Attaher (Tuareg Rebellion, 1960); Liu Xiaobo (Democratic China Protests, 1980s); and Guillermo Farinas (Cuban Censorship, 1990s)). Of course, you would question the rationale behind this, believing that the success of an idealist is the most critical parameter to judge. Naturally, the goal of an idealist is to succeed and execute the changes they have considered. However, that does not make one more or less of an idealist: it only makes one successful or unsuccessful (One could contend that the idealist may have succeeded in the goal of educating people about the cause and having his legacy upheld in the future - as has happened to Nana Sahib (India), Pablo Presbere (Costa Rica) and Tadeusz Kościuszko (Poland). Perhaps eventually all 'failed' idealists fall into this category.).

A person does not become less of an idealist because he failed, just as a person does not become less of a tennis player when they lose a match. That's only when they quit. Besides, many idealists have died so others could realise the ideals they lived for - from the tales of Jesus to the lore of Drona, from Joan d'Arc to Socrates. The sole goal is to bring change to society - never mind how. While many of us may not (and need not) have the courage to bring about revolutions of the mind, matter or material, those of us who do are idealists. And that leads to an exciting finding: most traditional 'bad guys' of history are just as idealistic as the revered 'good guys'. But how do we differentiate?

The Hypothesis of Morality

Morality is all about optics. The way society sees you is the way they judge you. So, what is the difference between what society considers good and bad in an idealist? Because it seems as though society changes its mind a lot on who is revered and who is not.

In addition, we must note that all of the originating idealists in any field are always welcomed negatively by society (For example, Vincent Van Gogh's Post-Impressionism. Negatively does not necessarily mean badly, it may also mean that people saw it as impractical/impossible). The only visible trend of difference between the retrospectively good and evil is the impact they cause. With multiple exceptions, the Idealist Hypothesis is a general rule through a somewhat predictable trend. It appears that 'good' movements usually start with hostility from what is considered society (hint: they aren't trying to please them). Such failed idealists include the Front de Libération Nationale Kanak et Socialiste in New Caledonia. This French overseas territory aimed to secure independence from France with disapproval from compatriots of the Kanak ethnicity itself. The 'good' idealists are usually regarded negatively by their target audiences due to their unrealistic expectations. However, these barriers are then usually overturned, and soon the movement gains exponential popularity. The progression of the stir from small to massive-scale may take years, but once the initial barrier is crossed, there is no stopping it. It's just a matter of dedication and time.

Take the example of Kalle Lasn, founder of Adbusters, the Canadian anti-consumerist magazine. He and the Adbusters crew were the force behind the Occupy Wall Street Movement of 2011. When suggested in February (as an article in Adbusters), it slipped out of public view until the movement gained attention for its planned September 17 protest to occupy the street. From June onwards, Occupy Wall Street started rising to the fore with significant momentum, supported by various anti-corporate groups - Day of Rage and Anonymous - to the extent that it took place. Despite its lack of an adequate (lasting) impact on the financial system, it fulfilled its goal of capturing the minds and attention of the 99%.

Alternatively, take the Indian independence movement, which originated in the various East and South Indian rebellions in the 18th century. Despite these isolated incidents until the First War of Independence in

1857, the movement remained stagnant, only seen in sporadic (faux?) nationalist outbursts. This dormancy remained until Bal Gangadhar Tilak proclaimed Indian independence his birth right, becoming India's first independence idealist. From here, the movement only expanded. Recognisable faces like Gandhi, Nehru, Abdul Ghaffar Khan and Jinnah rose with the Indian populace, dramatically acquiring what was previously impossible in four decades: independence.

Intriguingly, this trend is not limited to politics - although it is more pronounced there. Take science, for example, with the Copernican heliocentric theory. When theorised in the early 16th century, it lay dormant for many decades until scientific proof increased exponentially in the 17th century, especially with Galileo and Newton. Yet, he faced negative feedback from his contemporaries, especially from the then Catholic Pope and acclaimed astronomer Tycho Brahe.

Furthermore, this trend is remarkably consistent in music, religion, literature, and social sciences. Initially, people reacted negatively to Karl Marx's 'Das Kapital' thesis and the alt-rock band, The Velvet Underground & Nico's debut album. However, retrospectively, they set in motion huge impacts. They were all idealists.

It's Not Perfect

However, there are exceptions to this rule. Look at Adolf Hitler and the NSDAP. After a long gruelling struggle in war (WW1: Hitler served in German military forces) and prison, Hitler's NSDAP began to gain political power in the late 1920s. And then it clicked with the Germans. The growth was almost instantaneous from then on. People truly believed in their ideals or what they said they could attain as a nation. That was until their Idealism became a reality. Checking all the requirements for being a 'good idealist' by this trend, it is common knowledge that this was untrue: there's Benito Mussolini in Italy, Kim Il-Sung in North Korea and Mao Zedong in China.

No Morals for Idealists

Yet, why do I still say that idealism is not an ideology? If there is such a difference between the 'good' guys and the 'bad' guys, why include the latter anyway? Because, regardless of how history views them, they fulfilled the criteria to become idealists. Adolf Hitler or Robert Clive, Joseph Stalin or Alauddin Khilji, each of these notorious personalities had made substantial reforms previously thought unrealistic. The concept of Lebensraum and the Nazi takeover of Germany were all considered impossible - until they were done. Then again, Robert Clive led the East India Company's military conquest of Bengal. With his enormous forts and massive armies, Nawab Siraj-ud-Daulah was thought invincible until Clive, with treacherous trickery, cheated him out of his land. Joseph Stalin, born Dzhugashvili, was a Georgian comrade of the Bolsheviks.

He went against all odds and the express wishes of Lenin to take over the USSR, bringing about destructive change from collectivisation to political expansion. Finally, take Alauddin Khilji, who created a Hindu-subjugation regime after murdering his father-in-law and usurping power. These are power moves right out of an Idealist's playbook. But of course, they did not do society well.

However, Idealism does not presume such. There will always be the moral and the immoral. There are always idealists on either side, and most are on neither. This contradiction is just an extension of the dichotomy of human values. People do not fall into straightforward divisions of good and evil. Unfortunately, life isn't a maths problem, and there is no right or wrong. Times change everything and everyone, even opinions. Not even history can judge us well.

If history cannot judge us too, who are we to make such a profound ethical judgement so subjective? Besides, why does it matter? To each person, their beliefs are for the better of the world and society. To anti-vaxxers, they are a barrier against supposedly conspiratorial Big Pharma. To jihadis, a crusade against the seemingly ungodly modernism in the name of the Quran. To Naxals, the farmers' revolution against the bourgeois government of India. Yet, what makes them different from the rest of the idealists? Only their ideals.

Take this example.

> *You are about to embark upon the Great Jihad, toward which we have striven these many months. The eyes of the world are upon you. The hopes and prayers of Allah-fearing Muslims everywhere march with you. In company with our brave mujahids and fellow jihadis on other fronts, you will bring about the destruction of the American war machine, the elimination of Western tyranny over the oppressed people of Islam, and the security for ourselves in the Islamic world.*

NS-DAP Membership (1925-32)

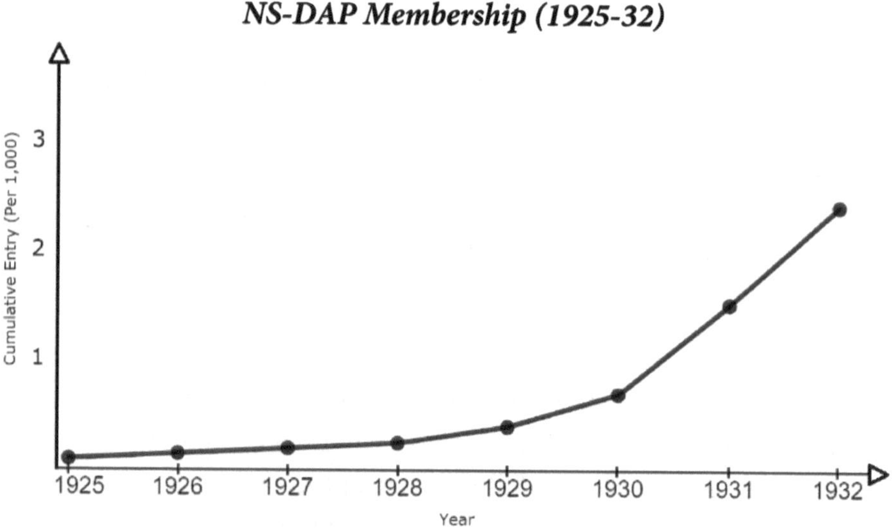

There is an exponential, albeit slow, rise in association with the NS-DAP, which is an exception to the Idealist Hypothesis.

Source: Bowling for Fascism: Social Capital and the Rise of the Nazi Party (Satyanath, et al.); Journal of Political Economy.

What did you think upon reading that last paragraph? "It appears to be a generic jihadi motivational speech, referring to the great jihad, Allah, Western tyranny and the American war machine". In many people, this may evoke recollections of ubiquitous suicide bombings, deaths, and perhaps loathing for the Islamic fundamentalist militancy.

However, take the actual unaltered excerpt of the speech delivered by General Dwight D Eisenhower ordering the invasion of Normandy in 1944.

> *You are about to embark upon the Great **Crusade**, toward which we have striven these many months. The eyes of the world are upon you. The hopes and prayers of **liberty-loving people** everywhere march with you. In company with our brave **Allies** and **brothers-in-arms** on other fronts, you will bring about the destruction of the **German** war machine, the elimination of **Nazi** tyranny over the oppressed people of **Europe**, and the security for ourselves in a **free** world.*

The language used by these radically different personalities is the same. The only words which differ are the ideals of each.

Faux-Jihadi	Eisenhower
Jihad	Crusade
Allah-fearing Muslims	Liberty-loving people
Mujahids	Allies
Jihadis	Brothers-in-Arms
Lands	Fronts
American	German
Western	Nazi
Islam	Europe
Islamic	Free

Society tells us that Eisenhower was/is right and that the jihadis were/are wrong. However, we cannot leave such ethical dilemmas to individuals since the only real difference between them is the ideals for which they fight. Perhaps it is best left to individual moral judgement to decide whether an action is evil or not. I probably share a worldview similar to billions of others - terrorism is wrong, get vaccinated, etc. Yet, this does not allow me the audacity to claim it is the final unyielding truth. Perhaps as Nietzsche argued, we should rise beyond just good and evil towards becoming 'Supermen'. Nobody is correct, and that includes us.

Society Needs a Villain

However, regardless of whether an idealist is good or bad, they are required. They constitute an indispensable part of society and its development. Every dragon who grows wings shows to other dragons that they can too, after all. Every community, to progress, needs both a hero and a villain. In some cases, the antagonist is a rival idealist. In contrast, it is sometimes an intangible entity (maybe more like Poverty than Hitler). Before you say this seems an oversimplification of matters and world history, let me remind you that progress need not always be idealistic. A realist's change in developing society is also possible, but there is virtually no difference. Change requires people. It doesn't matter what they wish to change - what matters is how it affects society. An idealist does not falter even if the whole world is against him. It doesn't matter whether he has one supporter or one million. The point is to spread the word and help people. Social labels are temporary; the impact you have is not. You should consider why people villainise you but never let it bog you down. Work in peace for your cause, knowing that even if history judges you as a villain, you have helped society move forward.

Look at all progress hitherto: be it the fight against inflation or colonial invasion, the recognition of cubism or progressive rock, or even the shock of Huxley's Brave New World or Darwin's theory of evolution, there is always an antagonist. Each of these discoveries was only possible because of the existence of exact rivals. There is nationalism because there was once imperial and colonial divisive rule. The Brave New World was only shocking because it directly hit out against the tight conservatism of Victorian-era morals. Darwin's theory, similarly, was only so influential as it directly countered the original religious belief of intelligent design, driving a final nail into the coffin of theism.

How To Be an Idealist in Society

An idealist wishes to change society primarily because they aren't happy with the one they live in. But there's a complication. In general, the present society tries hard to stay how it is. Everyone has their own deeply personal experience with this social inertia which rudely wakes them up. For me, it was when various 'educated' upper-class members slammed their doors on my face when I, a 14-year-old boy, came to ask for a few rupees for a campaign to save the environment. That woke me up. Maybe for you, it was at your school or your family. Either way, society didn't care about what anyone did to help it. But I realised it wasn't their fault or mine. It's a psychological trend: the status quo bias. The status quo bias is a disproportionate preference for things staying the way they are. The smaller a change to the status quo, the more ready we are to accept it. People weren't prepared to spare money for a cause they felt was lost/ of no use. For example, we may fight for a new parking spot on the street readily but not take up the crusade against the technological invasion of privacy.

Unfortunately, totalitarian governments have grossly exploited this psychological bias to consolidate control over the minds of their citizens. 'Life has always been this way, and we made it better.' This is how politicians have deluded all of North Korea, as had the post-war Soviet Union and Pakistan under various dictatorial figures. As you may have wondered, why don't people fight against such governments? A few people with all the weapons in the world cannot win against the rest of us without breaking us mentally. That is why it is vital to resist the seductive call of the status quo bias.

How do we overcome this? Firstly, we must all understand that our world is not perfect. You probably believe this, which is why you're still reading. Next, we must realise that any change can and will be done if you want it enough, from the slightest yet personal transformation to a global revolution. As you might have guessed, I lied. To see what you want the world to be, you must work for it. As soon as the problem crosses the popularly set barrier of a possible change, you become an idealist. And as soon as it does, many of you may give up, thinking about how you cannot commit either time, money or effort, possibly believing it unnecessary. Depending on your resistance levels and commitment, you may see society's war-footing as trying to stamp you out of existence. Sometimes, that is really the case. This social phenomenon is what I call the Invisible Foot.

The Invisible Foot

A Disclaimer: Many of you won't think of causes that society will so utterly degrade to this brink of stamping out (popularly, not governmentally).

In 1759, when we saw the first copy of Adam Smith's The Theory of Moral Sentiments, the invisible hand concept gained enormous popularity. So, what is the invisible hand? In economics, the invisible hand is a metaphor for how markets operate efficiently without any intervention. To Adam Smith, the father of capitalism, the invisible hand was the answer to everything: he believed that doing nothing was the most efficient outcome (socially and allocative). It pushed firms to supply products at specific prices and workers to demand certain prices (sometimes it would make firms leave the market too). It was a sort of let-it-be approach (technical term: laissez-faire).

The invisible foot is a similar metaphor. Here, it is a metaphor for how Idealist movements achieve popular efficiency. If a cause is socially useless/worsening, it is stamped out by the populace. For example, suppose most people don't want or care about your cause. In that case, society may make it difficult for your movement to continue - even personally. They may try to remove you from your job, put you in prison, et cetera. These actions will naturally increase the cost of following through. It is for you to decide whether to adhere to the stamping of the invisible foot or go on. Despite its flaws and problems, sometimes society is correct. Some movements are considered dangerous and unsavoury for a reason (E.g., Neo-Nazism, Paedophilia, Racism). Sometimes you have to shut up and stop trying to save the world. It may not be worth it.

We Are What We Change

Time is fragile, delicate, and so impressionable. Even the most minor change can derail or rescue our species' future. If a butterfly flapping its wings can cause cyclones on the other side of the Earth, your minute change can cause ripples through time. Imagine the number of lives your unrealistic change could touch, regardless of whether it is ever fulfilled. We are what we change. I hate to say it, but if you change nothing, you *are* nothing (in the balance settled in the future). I'm so sorry, and I apologise. What are you doing if you're not touching people's lives, helping them? We all have responsibilities (work, education, family, et cetera), but what makes you different from the other rats running the eternal rat race? What makes you a dragon amongst lizards? It is your life and yours to make alone. Will it be unimpactful? Or will it help people, however little recognition you get for it? Will you be an idealist?

Every idealist is crucial to society, just like every person. After all, we draw meaning in our life from our interactions with others (more on this in later chapters). Where would we be without Rousseau's inventive philosophy today? You wouldn't be reading this, for sure. But when all is said and done, we honour MLK Jr. for his brilliant ideas and not you (the general you) for yours. Why? Because one of you acted on your ideas and tried to make a better world. One of you was an idealist. The world isn't perfect, and we need to do a lot. Surely, you've noticed something wrong with the world. Get out of the chair and away from your comfort zone. It's time to change the world. But you need the right mentality - the art-connoisseur mentality.

PART II

The dragon looks up. Surely, what they see is a giant which aims to destroy the fire-breathing community. Naturally, the only thing to do is fight it off. But the dragon looks everywhere else - things are pretty blurry. They can't be sure of whether their talons are indeed talons. And those sharp, black claws were right in front of them. The tiny dragon really needed glasses - they needed clarity and vision! But where would they find that?

The Art Connoisseur Mentality

Or, Why You Should be Selective-Minded

'He was so narrow minded, he could see through a keyhole with both eyes.'

– Molly Ivins

Practically every other self-proclaimed life expert announces the need for his followers to keep an open mind at one point in their ''revolutionary courses''. Being open-minded is, in fact, a much-needed trope of the self-help industry (For more information see Bill Watterson's Calvin and Hobbes comic strip dated June 06, 1993). They ask everyone to be receptive to every idea. You know who I'm talking about - televangelists, spiritual gurus, the whole deal. While that is a touching sentiment, it is lamentably misplaced due to its lack of structure and benefit. We get hours of speeches about an open-minded nature, but who has an open mind? Is it mentally possible to be human and be objective? Probably not. We in the general public are terrible at being open-minded - we can't even agree on whether pineapple belongs on pizza. But what if we don't need to? What if we're wrong about being open-minded and reaching our innate human nature is the way forward?

The Mind is an Art Exhibit

Sherlock Holmes famously quipped, ''A mind is an attic: keep yours organised''. Be receptive to new ideas but don't let them into your mind. The open-minded non-confrontational approach to life will only result in ignorance. Your mind isn't closed; it's elite. Holmes was wrong: the mind is not an attic. It is an art exhibition.

As an art connoisseur, it is your job to choose what is essential to know and fits the rest of the art's theme. You must go over and consider everything you get. Perhaps some young street artist may provide you with the Picasso of the modern age. However, every time you get a new work of art, you must first check its authenticity (you don't want to put fake articles on display, do you?). Then you must check whether they make sense with the rest of the art you already have, or do they make more sense than some other artwork you already had? If it fits with no rivals, it works. Otherwise, you consider both and decide which fits the theme the most.

Designing an Art Exhibit

This scheme is precisely how one's mind should work. Like an art connoisseur, you should get information from all sources (like *this* art connoisseur). However, before just blindly adding it in, you must follow the five steps the exhibit above does:

1. Authenticate the information.
2. Ensure it makes sense with your information and logic.
3. If it opposes the information you already know, see if it makes sense to replace it.
4. Otherwise, add it if it makes a good addition to your information.
5. In the absence of fulfilling these factors, reject it.

How To Not Be Stupid

The ACM implies that you must admit your ignorance and accept that nothing you know is absolute. You've been wrong about something before, I'm sure. Admit it. 'Admit. Adapt. Overcome.' Fallibility is indeed a vital component of the ACM. When you don't acknowledge how your beliefs can be wrong, you limit your development because you have a big ego. Don't be stupid. Nevertheless, it is also wrong to not debate an authentic piece of information if it does not make sense to the rest of your mind. Maybe you've found something others have not.

This scheme may seem quite familiar to those who learnt high school science. After all, it's the scientific method!

1. Observe
2. Question
3. Try to explain
4. Test the explanation
5. Refine and replicate

Question Everything

You must maintain the attitude of a sceptic within your mind. If you don't ask someone else about your new beliefs, at least ask yourself. When confronted with a new piece of information, you must ask repeated questions and compare what you believe is the answer with what you already know. Then, when you are sufficiently convinced or otherwise, you can choose to accept or reject the information. However, you mustn't fear admitting ignorance, for it is, after all, in your mind. There is nobody in there who can judge you other than you.

Questioning everything is the only way to get essential information about your surroundings and world. Moreover, questions are very influential - they can collapse countries and resurrect rulers. Just think about young Karl Marx questioning the general line of economic thinking. That led to a century of revolution. We'll look at the power of questions in a later chapter ('Why?').

Doublethink

The ACM is a short but essential piece of the exemplary idealist. However, a definitive psychological problem now occurs—holding opposing thoughts simultaneously. Or, as Orwell coined the term in his book nineteen-eighty-four, the practice of "doublethink". This paradox is usually solved by nonsensical reconciliation in humans or cognitive dissonance. Or, in simpler words, we think up whatever insane excuse we can to avoid the conflict of ideals which rages within our minds.

According to F Scott Fitzgerald in his story "The Crack-Up", this ability of humans to doublethink is a sign of "first-rate intelligence". He joked about the need to change things while seeing that it was all hopeless: a pervasively negative view, but one held by so many. The best analogy of such seemingly irreconcilable theories appears in science - the classical theory of mechanics and the quantum theory of mechanics. Or maybe that time when you ate those oily burgers, knowing that they'll increase your cholesterol levels. What was your explanation then?

On the other hand, there is the understanding of science and the belief in religion. As any high schooler should ideally know, biology tells us that for a child to be born, their parents must have sex. Thus, if these high schoolers came across a woman claiming to be pregnant while still possessing her virginity, they would laugh her out of the room. However, those same Christians amongst them hold beliefs in millennia-old religious books telling them of Mary and Joseph who had a child Jesus without losing their virginity. We'll look at the strange case of religion in a later chapter ('God and Religion').

Other less controversial examples of this dichotomy include lucky charms, which do not affect people's lives, yet people use them. How do people with even such high educational qualifications succumb to this? Because they justify their beliefs and prioritise. Perhaps religious scientists genuinely believe that God is behind all of science (For example: Francis Collins and Tadeusz Pacholczyk). Perhaps mathematicians with rabbit's foot necklaces truly believe that inductively the rabbit's foot causes luck and does not correlate to it. More probably, they prioritise differently in different circumstances. For example, they may prefer science in their employment but religion in times of distress.

So how do we solve this paradox? We don't. We cannot: this is a more accurate answer. We subconsciously do this since we cannot know everything. Despite knowing that, many of us hold contradictory beliefs - be it the knowledge of climate change yet buying cars or understanding blue light eye damage yet using screens quite a lot. We often prioritise beliefs as a justification. Perhaps you feel that a vehicle is needed in the present to live. Thus, you cannot worry about the future at that moment. So, all you can do as an idealist with the ACM is try your best to minimise their chasm. First, we can sort out lower relevance beliefs to prevent additional mental strain due to cognitive dissonance. It's all a matter of priority: do you prioritise your happiness from eating a burger over your long-term health? Thinking in these terms often makes our decisions easier.

Conclusion

So, with foreknowledge of the ACM and idealism, a new pillar of human philosophy remains. What is our motivation to follow the ACM or idealism? Do we have a purpose or meaning? Is this because of some supernatural force or not? The answer is relatively short and straightforward, but it may not be what you expect, as you see in the next chapter.

PART III

The dragon could see clearly now. And what they saw disturbed them greatly. Death, ruin and giants ran amok in his homeland. Before them, a giant walked to join in on this rampage. There were too many problems, and they were just one dragon. What was the point? Why were they here? In the tiny dragon's head ran the only question which mattered: why did they have to help? What was the meaning of it all anyway? In the end, they'd be crushed under the feet of a giant anyway. Perhaps it was of no use to save such a community. What was the purpose of their life? What was the meaning?

Life – No Purpose, All Meaning

Or, Why We Don't Need a Purpose to Live

'The meaning of my life is to help others find meaning in theirs.'
— Victor Frankl

For centuries, philosophers and preachers, scientists and songwriters have tried to unlock the purpose and meaning of life. And hopefully, so have you. For what reason do I exist? Why do we need to grow the wings of a dragon? What is the meaning of this existence? These deep questions have many answers - from nihilistic to scientific, utilitarian to theological. I'll explain what those complex terms mean in a moment. Before that, we must clarify what purpose and meaning imply as terms. The purpose of a person is their function and the reason for their birth. It is consistent from their birth to death. Simply put, purpose implies the reason a person was born. Meaning, on the contrary, discusses what life is to you? What's the point of living? How are we meaningful as individuals and units of a society?

Bound by Morals

Religious philosophers believe that the purpose of our lives is to live life within the constraints of the Creator's edicts. Those edicts happen to come to us in the form of religious books and scriptures such as the Talmud, Quran, Vedas and others. Do you agree/follow these books? Think about why you do. Now, the standard description of the Creator is - benevolent, omnipotent, omniscient and such. A strange and impossible combination (if you know everything that is going to happen, you can't stop it from happening despite having supreme power). If we were to leave this for the moment, let us look at a young IT professional with vast experience in natural language processing, machine learning and coding. He programmes various chatbots and robots with Artificial Intelligence for one purpose.

Believers vs Non-Believers when asked their opinion on the statement: 'In my opinion, life does not serve any purpose'.

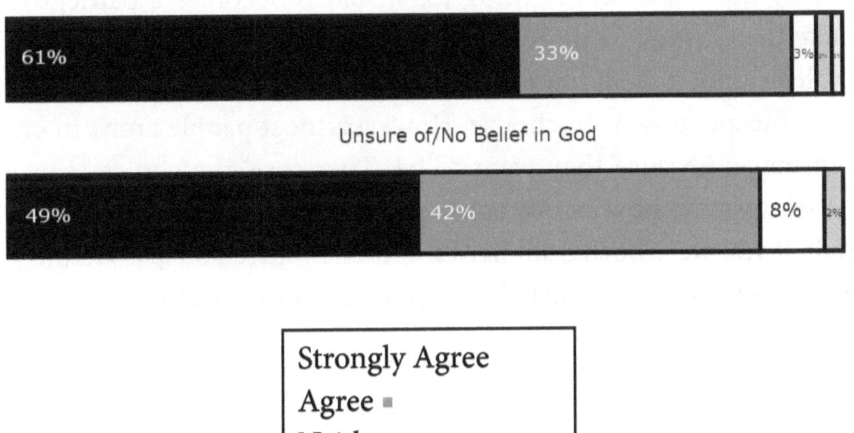

Source: Stephen Cranney, "Do People Who Believe in God Report More Meaning in Their Lives? The Existential Effects of Belief". Journal for the Scientific Study of Religion.

So, they can praise him. Something would be wrong with the person who surrounds themselves with self-praising artificial intelligence. What would you call such a person? Most would call him a narcissist, though intelligent. Now replace the programmer with God and his bots with human beings. Is God a massive narcissist? Of course, that assumes that God exists (which we will address in the chapter 'God and Religion').

Or, assume this same IT professional creates an AI to entertain him by making them fight each other (as intelligent chatbots today do) and enact dramas. All that pointless suffering, misery and death. Why? To him, it's unreal: nobody's dying because they're just toys to him. Still, the idea doesn't feel right. It's our world in a nutshell. God is a lonely sadist. But hold on! That's not the end of our religious story. Maybe you're a Zoroastrian or a Setian - a religious dualist.

Now, dualists believe that there are two morally opposed supernatural powers - usually a 'good' power and an 'evil' power. So then, the purpose of humans is to serve one of the two. Now humans are just mercenaries, choosing their side and fighting for it. Earth becomes a battleground. It's like the Cosmic Cold War again! It seems as though all the world's a battleground, and all the men and women are merely soldiers. By this means, our purpose is to choose. However, most people aren't in crime, for instance, because they want to be. Therefore, the choice is usually not their own. So how can you choose or change sides as the religion lets you do if you were born a soldier of one side? Since you also define your purpose at birth, the dualist philosophy becomes tautological.

Finally, let's look at the pantheistic view of purpose. Here, God is one with the universe; he is a part of everyone and everything. Perhaps the most suitable explanation in pop culture of pantheism is Star Wars with the Force. Now, the Force is impersonal and has no character of its own. It unites everything, good and evil, but it does not expect anything. Pantheism additionally believes that thus, the universe may well have created God along with us. Hence, God is not our Creator, and therefore we were not a creation. So, pantheistically speaking, we should not have a God-given purpose - because nobody created us.

The Problem with Pleasure

Next, there is the utilitarian perspective. A very philosophical term, but fear not. It's pretty simple. This sect of philosophers tells us that perhaps our sole purpose is seeking pleasure, and that's why we were created/evolved. Perhaps the dragon doesn't need wings - unless they're in pain. Firstly, we must differentiate between creationist utilitarianism and evolutionary utilitarianism. While these creationists believe that

God created us for pleasure, evolutionists believe that we evolved for this reason. But what exactly is pleasure? Is pleasure only the happiness of the individual in question, or does it involve that of society as well? There are plenty of examples of a clash between the two - look at the penal code.

If we were to admit that pleasure is purely personal, the religious amongst us would differ (with good reason). To state that pleasure is subjective is to condone thievery, murder, and other such crimes. Is it truly a person's purpose if he receives joy from rape? By saying so, are we condoning the same? At this moment, creationists would disagree and state that it involves the happiness of society as well. And that's the argument for religion: a social order. Religion binds us by its constraints. In this case, we would anticipate that living in a religious code would provide maximum societal happiness. Unfortunately, the more people are a part of a religion, the more complicated it gets. Humans tend to differ, even if they have the same morals or identify with the same group. In addition, greater complexity causes factions to emerge and split, thus causing further discord.

Why are there approximately five thousand religions with hundreds of breakaway groups from Christianity? If we were to live by a 2000-year-old religious edict, it would not make much sense and would inhibit progress as it does already. Hence, by the very existence of religion, specifically scriptures, society cannot reach its maximum pleasure. That's another paradox. Indeed, serving an old rock with letters cannot be the purpose of life. No human can think about life thousands of years into the future, let alone a few hundred. It's mind-boggling and hopeless (I discuss why in the bonus chapter 'Predicting the Future'). Thus, religious society inherently reduces happiness over time. If things change, but we don't, how can we continue to live by these edicts?

Imagine someone telling your great-great-grandfather the secret to happiness is to farm. So, he sells everything and buys a plot of land to farm, and your family becomes farmers. Then, however, you start seeing the world is changing around you - huge skyscrapers, property taxes, government intervention, the internet, and so much more. Gradually, the world bogs you down because you follow the same practices your great-great-grandfather did. There is no happiness without change.

Why Are We Happy

Let's talk about evolutionary utilitarianism. The base unit of evolution and every species on the planet is the gene. In his book *The Selfish Gene*, Richard Dawkins explained that we are all hosts for genes to pass on copies and survive the longest in gene pools. So, survival or existence is the most apt explanation of our evolutionary purpose. More accurately, it would be procreation/attempting to procreate. Hence, the person with the maximum fertility and sexual partners (choosing similarly fertile sexual partners, not to mention luck) would have succeeded in their purpose. However, we are not having sex with someone in every free moment (I imagine you are reading this book). Why? Why don't we?

We have attained an environmental and internal means to inhibit our genetics and rebel against them. A possible conjecture is the existence of a gene which does precisely this in our bodies. That would mean we cannot have evolved the purpose of having pleasure, for clearly, evolution has endowed us with the ability to rebel against our genes. There's only one other theory about purpose from the evolutionary utilitarian perspective - mere existence. Is our purpose just existing? Perhaps we haven't evolved for pleasure, but we seek happiness from our existence? Are you happy to be human, or are you happy because you're human?

Do Not Misunderstand

One more common definition of purpose is doing things about which you are passionate. However, just as we had defined purpose earlier, this is a tautology. Do you feel that you have a purpose in life? You may think it is your job, children, or religion. However, if you were to go back a decade or two, do you still have those same priorities and purposes? If you go back to your childhood, do you still possess the same purpose? The answer would presumably be no. You have donned different personas and purposes at other points in time. Are they purposes by the definition of a purpose - constant and immutable? No. These are short-term purposes (from a whole life's perspective). They are identities. And identities change. That soccer kid from school may now be a business manager. That soccer player you met long ago may now be an author writing about their adventures. These goals are simply temporary.

Why Do We Exist?

So, what is our purpose? Nothing, or merely existing. Our life is without purpose, but not necessarily without meaning. Imagine, once again, art on display in an exhibition. Art serves no purpose or function: its very existence is enough for the world. There is no need for it to begin cooking or doing the laundry to fulfil its life. Yet, it has intrinsic meaning. But, of course, different people interpret it differently.

Humans are like art pieces. They serve no purpose yet have inherent meaning gained from their interactions with others and themselves (for every person has many complexities and personas). So likewise, a person's life gains meaning from their interactions with others and how they touch their lives. This understanding of life is an integral portion of idealism too. We draw meaning from the impact we have on other people and from the impact other people have on us. We are, after all, art.

So, Are We Nothing?

Does this all mean that we are nothing? That we, me and you as individuals, amount to nothing? Were the nihilists right? Does nothing matter? Are we completely insignificant, with no purpose or meaning? The first myth to dispel is our insignificance. We are significant, defined by our life's meaning or its impact. For example, Gandhi's interactions and impressions of other people led to the independence of Bangladesh, India and Pakistan.

Similarly, Hitler's interactions and beliefs about other people led to World War II. However, nihilists often look at the bigger picture. How are we significant in context with the universe and the infinitely extending past and future?

The universe is either completely lonely or filled with life. There is no point in the middle. Either there is no other life (and we are alone), or there is boundless life (just waiting to be discovered). As I stated before, our existence alone flips off the universe's laws if we are alone. Even if we aren't, our actions impact the volatile future. Everything we do is of the utmost significance - from our morals to sexual behaviour. All systems at a deeper level are inherently chaotic and thus are party to Lorenz's butterfly effect. Following chaos theory, even the slightest change in initial conditions can cause large ripples later. For example, you only exist reading this book because of the chance sexual deviance of an obscure non-sapiens human (Explained later).

After all, your whole personality is an interaction between the world inside you with the one outside you. Even the most random memories, such as tripping on rocks, can have meaningful consequences in the future (it's sometimes unexpected and sometimes deliberate what memories we remember). Suppose we are truly alone in this universe. In that case, everything we do now will significantly change the universe's future (perhaps it defines whether we colonise galaxies or not, passing the great filter).

The Meaning of Life

Thus, we derive meaning in life from our impact on other people's lives. The very interactions we have with other people define who we are and who they are. We are worth what we do for others while we become what others do to us. That is all life is. Just because we were born for nothing doesn't mean we cannot be anything! Think about the freeing relief of having no purpose or task to fulfil. It's like that little free time you have (real free time) where all you want to do is stretch your legs, relax, listen to music or do your sin of choice. Life is an endless race: but at least you were born to do nothing - not a job, not for a God or any idea. You were born to be you, and you're doing a phenomenal job (despite what others may say).

The dragon may not have any purpose, but they derive meaning from their impact on others. How much of an impact do they have as a fire-breathing lizard? With wings, they are truly free - with a power to change unlike before.

We exist because of accidental molecular collisions. However, this does not mean that we squander the solitary opportunity we have on this Earth wallowing in self-doubt. Indeed, it is just because of our lack of purpose that we are free to choose our path and define our destiny. Or are we? Is there such a thing as free will, and does it matter? What about the Creator? Perhaps we need to reconsider how free we are.

PART IV

The tiny dragon continued on their quest to raise an army of dragons to fight off the giants, now armed with meaning. Still, some doubts plagued them. Every time they spat out a fireball, watched another young dragon grow wings, or just lived, they felt tiny insecurity. What if everything that happened was meant to happen? Was there any point in their Idealist crusade, if it was all scripted? Should they give up now and let the giants trample them? In short, did they have free will, or was this sadistic entertainment for the Gods.

Free Will (Or not)

Or, How Does Free Will Affect Us

'Life is like a game of cards. The hand you are dealt is determinism; the way you play it is free will.'

– Jawaharlal Nehru

Are you voluntarily reading this? Do you have the ability to stop - and if you do, was it your choice? Take a moment and think. Do you feel like you can choose how your life unfolds? Or is it pre-planned? This exercise tells us what we think about free will - our ability to choose any way we like, free of influence and constraints. What is the point of doing what is bound to happen?

The Hypothetical Death of Free Will

Imagine a hypothetical society that has completely mapped the human genome. All the more fascinating is the new power they have: the ability to edit the human gene sequence fully. Naturally, society is ecstatic - they decide to implement this technology immediately. Scientists in league with social scientists and experts come together to create an efficient and elegant way to help society develop. How so? They manipulate people's genetics and environment.

Take, for instance, a boy born into this society who needs him to be a soldier. He is born with significant genetic potential in his strength. However, he has lesser intelligence, in comparison, to increase compliance. He will then grow up with a patriotic family in a neutral-nationalist neighbourhood. As he grows up on a diet of patriotism, self-sacrifice and schooling, his brain evaluates his loves and strengths - thus wanting to join the army. Naturally, as he was born to be a part of the army, he gets into the military, reaching peak job satisfaction.

In addition, this society creates another person sexually attracted to the army man (amongst other things). As we made them for each other, they will 'inevitably' find each other and marry - this would peak marital and sexual satisfaction alongside social utility. To sum up, progress, happiness, pleasure, joy: everything of value in life is yours, thanks to a fascinating society (but they don't need to know that). Would you live in this society or not?

These paragraphs describe a thought experiment that may become a reality in the future. Until now, philosophical discussions on free will have been obscure and unimportant. However, soon we may face a crossroads like this - to choose eternal progress and happiness or free will (possibly). Of course, that is believing we do have free will in the first place. Would people react? People generally don't care about this philosophical discourse, even if it affects them. As explained previously, humans excel in holding two conflicting ideas simultaneously - free will and God. So, what's different from what we have today? Another view, however, shows a world of difference. Naturally, as the world draws closer to this society, we must understand where we draw the line for sacrifice.

What Do the Philosophers Think?

So, what is free will? Depending on who you ask, there are many definitions of free will. According to Thomas Aquinas, all humans are pre-programmed with specific desires and goals. However, the choice of reaching them is an individual's choice - their free will. He added that God, being the first cause, has caused this - and the guy who gives you your 'purpose'. We will try and avoid God wherever possible - and we already talked about purpose. Next, David Hume's definition is the ability to perform a particular action or not if the will wants. So, this will be due to the desires and goals of the agent.

On the other hand, Gottfried Leibniz believed that all choices were made by an omnipotent, omniscient God, keeping in mind the individual's choices - compatibilism. But then, there's Democritus (another Greek, yes) tells us that all actions happen due to their past state of affairs and the laws of physics - we have no free will. And just as we're getting comfy with that - Nietzsche viciously tears apart the concept of free will, telling us that every thought of ours exists because of an external cause. So, there is no free will in Nietzsche's nihilism. Philosophy is such a mess of ideas. Let's move on.

Response and Circumstance

It's time for my opinion. So, our genetics defines our physical characteristics - our hair colour or speed. While we can alter and improve many, they cannot move past a particular genetic barrier or genetic potential. For example, suppose a person is born with flat feet. Regardless of the number of training sessions they can, they will not be able to run as fast as another similar, equally trained person without flat feet. But that's not all: our genetics influence our behaviour as well. Sexual preferences, for instance, are linked to our genetics too. Thus, they affect how we behave around people who fit our sexual preferences.

In addition, if we add the factor of the environment in which we grew up and are currently in, we find ourselves constrained by a larger box. A person who grows up learning Xhosa, for instance, will have a more challenging time learning Kannada than someone who might have learnt Tamil growing up.

Thus, our genetics and environment define our choices. Many of you might disagree: believing that gut feeling of freedom. Let's take a step back and look at Hume's points on free will: we should be able to act otherwise, not only the desire. If there are two people in question, a free man (Free Will), and a jailed man (Jailed Will), it is only Free Will who has, eponymously, free will. While Jailed Will may wish to be in jail, but it does not mean it is an act of free will. He has no other choice. He could not get out of jail regardless.

Similarly, even if I don't wish to have a scaly skin, I cannot grow it - implying my genetics constrains me. That's not the free will to not develop scales. Additionally, like most humans, I cannot think my thoughts in anything but a language. So, my environment constrains me.

Behaviour Genetics

The field of behaviour genetics studies the impact of an organism's genetic composition on its behaviour. Though fascinating, with its sadly controversial history of eugenics and wildly Nazi/racist "proofs", behaviour genetics was shunned in the modern era. However, it is finally reawakening in its purely scientific form alongside evolutionary psychology. From this new research, there is sufficient proof for three conclusions in behavioural genetics:

1. Genetics influences all behavioural traits (The apparent conclusion for something called 'behaviour genetics').
2. Environmental factors tend to make members of the same family more different than similar.
3. Ageing increases the relevance of genetics to behaviour.

Multiple studies on twins have proven that they don't have the same psyche despite having the same genetic factors. The environment is vital to constraining our behaviour as well. Well-documented examples include the CHRNA5 gene in humans. This gene encodes a nicotinic acetylcholine receptor protein, making humans more conducive to smoking. Similarly, the East-Asian ALDH2 is an aldehyde dehydrogenase enzyme protein that makes people more conducive to acute alcoholic intoxication. Let's stick to simple stuff: a gene which makes us more likely to smoke and a gene which makes us more intoxicated by alcohol. And there are many such genes which influence in many ways - both little and large.

In that case, our feelings, too, are determined by our genetics and environment. Therefore, we only possess a certain amount of free will in this theory. Building on the views of Aquinas and Democritus while noting Hume's condition and Nietzsche's understanding of thought, I see a new theory forming.

1. All beings exist because of previous beings (cell theory, pretty self-explanatory there).
2. All beings have genes (be they natural or not).
3. All beings live within an environment - their family, friends, teachers, colleagues, et cetera.
4. Since all beings inherit genes from their parents and their tendencies from their environment, they have no free will in choosing their personality.
5. However, their actions are their own, which involve interactions between three fields of an experience - genes, environment and circumstance.
6. Humans have no free will in genes and environment but abundant free will by circumstance.

So, Are We Free?

Let's come back to the initial thought experiment. From one perspective, there is no real difference between the amount of free will we have then and now. The difference only exists in who is deciding our fate. That is, in all ways, a technocracy of social science, science and AI. But then again, we would be the happiest humans not because of the absence of pain but due to the existence of satisfaction: humans cannot attain happiness without pain. We would be listless, apathetic and stagnant.

However, this society has pain, but with pleasure in the end. It is like a romantic movie - we know it has a happy ending. Yet what is the difference? We still only possess our minimal circumstantial free will. Even if humans knew about this plan, would they try to change it? As mentioned previously, humans have proven their prowess at simultaneously keeping multiple contradictory thoughts. Thus, we will believe we control what we do and know how we are genetically and environmentally conditioned. Perhaps this little cognitive dissonance is worth the benefit.

On the contrary, this view does not regard circumstantial free will as relatively insignificant in deciding the impact of a scenario on a person and their reaction at that moment. It is what leads to the response and effect. For example, imagine a person born in this society choosing to drive left at an intersection instead of right. As a specific *Doctor Who* episode showed us, this can make a difference - Lorenz's chaos theory in effect. That person may survive a car crash, change their personality, or live by not choosing to go right. Thus, in many ways, circumstantial free will is just as significant as environmental and genetic free will since our experiences define our personality. So, in this world, regardless of how much control exists, we will always have a considerable amount of free reign over ourselves.

Another view goes that this is not the end of a happy tale but the beginning of a dystopian novel. Just as Huxley's *Brave New World* looked ideal yet unsettling, this world is a living nightmare. If the government coordinates everything, it affects far more than our overall choices. If the government wishes to impact us on a large scale, it must start trivially. According to Rutger Bregman's *Humankind: A Hopeful History*, terrorists don't get motivated to blow themselves up from reading arcane texts and propaganda - they get it from their friends and family, their habits, etc. Thus, such a society would either not work or would place the power to control a significant portion of even our circumstantial free will.

Conclusion

Perhaps this requires more deliberation. Every day we make decisions which give our governments and corporations more and more control of our circumstantial and environmental free will. As a member of Gen Z, I have enjoyed an increasingly controlled environment. From the "random" YouTube recommendations I get to the "random" advertisements I get on websites everywhere; we have let go of our most precious commodity - chaos. When a few people can manipulate chaos, they get absolute control over us - then we finally lose our free will.

But what about God? Many philosophers have believed in God over the centuries, arguing both sides of free will on his part. Yet, is God still relevant in today's world? Does he define our free will too? What about religion? How do they equate with the idealist philosophy? Let's find out.

PART V

The dragon, amidst existential crisis, was met by another of his kind. This dragon had the shine of novelty and the arrogance of morality. Our tiny dragon cowered in his presence. 'You are in consternation, my child,' he exclaimed. The dragon nodded, discussing their issues with their purpose and morality. The new dragon pompously flexed his scales. 'The answer to all your worries is one word. God,' he said with complete conviction. 'And we need your help,' he continued, 'There, look! There are the ones who stand between us and utopia.' The tiny dragon thought he was pointing at the giants. He put on his new ACM glasses. He was pointing at an inferno of dragons. 'They do not believe in our Lord,' he said, getting agitated, 'It is their immorality which stands between you and the giants. Fight them for it the will of God!'

The Harmony of the Godless

Or, Why We Don't Need God

> *'Religion began when the first scoundrel met the first fool.'*
>
> – *Voltaire*

Every culture everywhere has believed in some supernatural entity - sometimes more than just one. Indians, Greeks, Zulu or Hun: this affinity for divinity seems to spring eternal. I hope you didn't buy that. For centuries, theists, philosophers and historians have tried to convince us that every culture manifested some belief in God. This convergence was supposed to 'prove' the existence of God. But, of course, it was merely due to cultural exchange. Some isolated groups never developed a sense of religion or God. Take the example of the Piraha people of the Amazon. They have never had a concept of a divine entity of any sort. Although Christian proselytisers tried to convert them, they failed. The one question the tribe asked the missionaries remains poignant. What is the physical evidence of God or Jesus? Nothing? Welcome to Atheism.

Ancient Atheists

Atheism has a long line of belief, just like theism. The Vaisheshika school of Hindu thought didn't have a God (they just disproved it). And then Jainism denied having any creator-God. Unlike how theistic historians make it out, God was not a universal idea. The largely Euro-centric version of history has flawed our perception of religion - many Asiatic religions were not God-based. Instead, they discussed the spiritual nature of many scientific and moral hypotheses. There are many such philosophies and beliefs - the Charvaka founded by Brihaspati, Ghosala's

Ajivaka sect, the Mimamsa school, the Epicureans, the Sophists, and so many others.

Average Change in Religiosity (2007-2019)

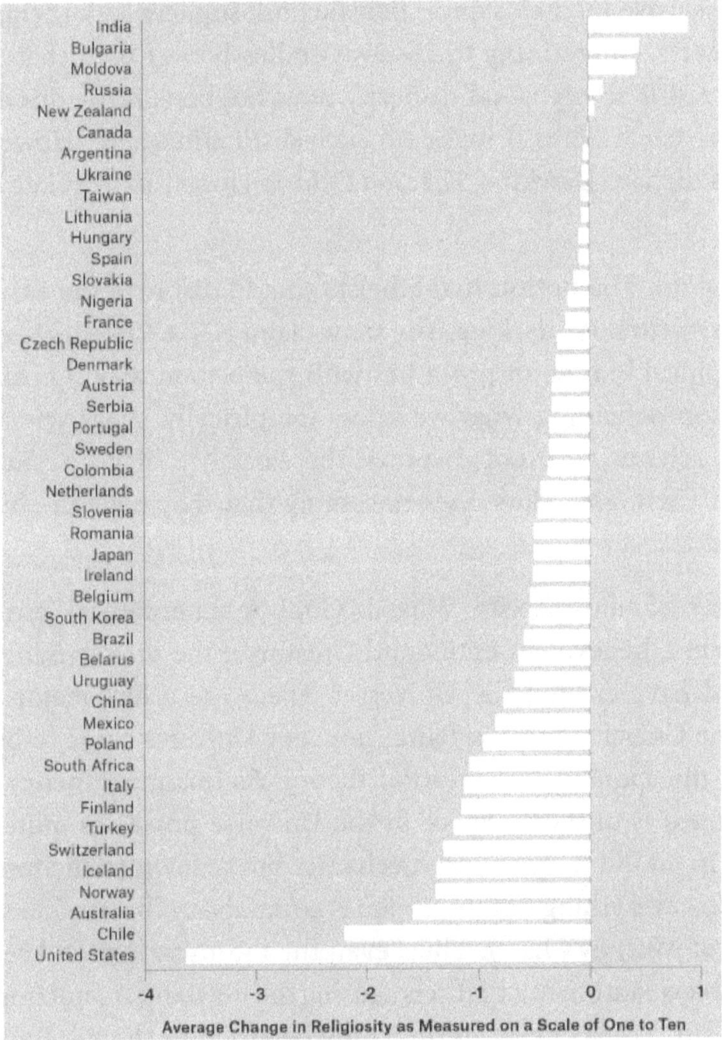

Source: Inglehart, Ronald F.

We are scientists by nature - that is how we gained control of the world around us, making us who we are. Where would we be without our interest in the outside world? Apes on the tree? Extinct? Curiosity is the core human value - and atheism is its clear offspring.

The God Who Obeyed Newton

In philosophy, there is a tradition of separating God from science. The sheer stupidity of this distinction is evident. By removing the very facts which disprove their existence, theistic philosophers lock themselves in ivory towers, entertaining themselves endlessly over the debate of God. However, this science-God disparity does not benefit the discussion of God's existence. Thus, I make no such distinction here. However, one can read Richard Dawkins' *The God Delusion* for an appropriate disproof of God.

But hang on. The notion that atheists should disprove the existence of the supernatural is hilarious. The same claim is like Russell's teapot. The philosophical burden of proof lies with the person making claims, not the person defending what we know (empirically, that's science). Just because scientists cannot disprove the existence of a celestial teapot between Earth and Mars does not imply that they have the burden of rebuttal.

Okay, let's humour theists. What is God? A supernatural, omniscient, omnipotent, benevolent entity and Creator of the universe/life. Firstly, can God have created the Universe? There are a few major theories about the Universe pre-Big Bang (how our Universe came to be). First, there is the spontaneous creation theory. As quantum theory tells us, nothingness is unstable. Space in the Universe possesses quite a lot of energy. In addition, quantum mechanics bows down to the totalitarian principle - everything not forbidden is compulsory (basically a scientific version of Murphy's Law). Thus, even the most random and seemingly impossible quantum fluctuations causing the Big Bang are not impossible. Indeed, since the concept of time only begins after the Big Bang, to us, the Big Bang seems to happen in a flash.

Speaking of time is the Hartle-Hawking state theory of pre-Big Bang cosmology. According to this theory, if the Universe began from nothing, perhaps the Universe did not have an origin as we think of it. Instead, maybe the Universe was a space-time singularity which first led to an expansion in space and then time. Alternatively, the string theory and ekpyrotic models of the Big Bang provide us with ideas relating to random quantum collisions causing the Universe to exist.

Now, if we assume that the Universe began from nothing, there are two alternative theories. First, the Brane cyclic model tells us that these previously mentioned quantum collisions occur periodically, causing periodic bangs and crunches (Where the Universe shrinks). But, none of these theories allows for anything before the Universe - which must exist for a God to exist. So, the eternal inflation theory tells us that universal inflation ends randomly but without a Big Crunch. Here, each endpoint leads to a bubble or pocket universe. That means God is irrelevant. With or without God, this Universe would exist.

In every possible way, the Universe comes to exist without the need for a Creator. So why assume he was the Creator? However, some may dispute that the conditions of the scientific constants that define life's existence are too fine-tuned to be random. However, according to the totalitarian principle, it was bound to happen. It does not matter if he was or was not. Let's account for the possibility that he was a by-product of the Big Bang. He created life, not the Universe.

Religion and Its Major Subcategories

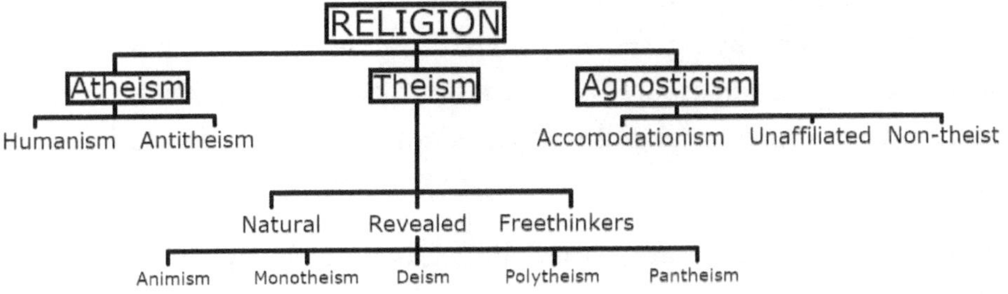

Atheism		Theism		Agnosticism	
Antitheism	E.g. Richard Dawkins	Natural	E.g. Aristotle	Accommodationism	E.g. Charlie Chaplin
Humanism	E.g. Isaac Asimov	Freethinker	E.g. Isaac Newton	Unaffiliated	E.g. James Joyce
		Animism	E.g. Nick Herbert	Non-theism	E.g. BR Ambedkar
		Monotheism	E.g. Pope Francis		
		Deism	E.g. Neil Armstrong		
		Polytheism	E.g. Mohandas Gandhi		
		Pantheism	E.g. Albert Einstein		

The God Who Was Newton

What if this Creator did not create the Universe but solely life on Earth? That leads to two types of Gods—the impersonal and the personal. A personal god micromanages the affairs of humanity, answering prayers and whatnot. Unfortunately for theists, there is no personal god. Scientists would have noted the same if we could get rain and other such phenomena by prayer. Any anecdotes about having your prayers 'answered' can be attributed to the fallacy of weak induction. Perhaps there was an impersonal god who does not care about life, studies it, or finds it entertaining.

However, the chances are rather dim. Once again, by the totalitarian principle, life was bound to happen on Earth by quantum fluctuations. Then again, what is the literal point of believing in this God who does not care what we do with our lives? At its bare minimum, the deist god is that random quantum fluctuation. What does it matter to believe in it? Thus, the deist God dies not of disproving but of irrelevance.

Pantheism leaves us with a fascinating case. All science becomes a work of God, believing that God is identical to the world. No wonder many prominent scientists of the 20th century expressed a belief in pantheism. However, just like in the case of deism, this makes the pantheistic God irrelevant. Suppose one believes that God is science or that science is God (the former implies that God is science itself while the latter means that science is a work of God). Why does it matter whether you appease this God or not? Some pantheists may say the world is illusory, the acosmic approach, and only God is real.

This approach is reminiscent of Pascal's Wager. Pascal once told us that there was a chance that God existed and another that he did not. Would we prefer believing in him and finding out he didn't exist or vice versa? Naturally, many would say 'believe he exists'. However, would your supposed God want that? If this God you believe in is a benevolent entity, as you suggest, would he prefer you doubt his existence or blindly believe it?

The Unholy Acts of Holy Men

So, let's try to understand the relationship between God and humanity. What has God decreed, and what has man done? That depends on who you ask. Prophet Muhammed told his followers that he came with a message from God, just like the many prophets and Christ before him. So, he led them to conquest, creating a prosperous caliphate which would one day become the centre of the world, spanning Spain to India (the Umayyad Caliphate). Or trust the ancient Hindus who believed that repeated rituals, chants and colour would summon the Gods. So, they created a synthesis of thought and shared knowledge to write some of the most profound pieces of philosophy from the period (the Upanishads). Religion has had its share of epiphanies. However, what allows you to tell someone God sent you into the right religion but not your counterpart - perhaps the Serer or Judaism? Faith is full of holes. Those holes have spurred millennia of war and genocide as they do today.

All of that is under the guise of religious idealism. Today, religious idealism contributes to much of the world's news. In every religion, we find fringe elements contributing to fanaticism, committing disturbing atrocities in God's name. From the anti-missionary peaceful Hindu thought, we have the orange army of anti-conversionists and xenophobes. Islam, the religion of unity under the spiritual belief, gives us the militant Salafist jihadis proclaiming an Islamic state. The faith of tranquillity and acceptance, Buddhism, gives us the notorious Japanese doomsday cultists who orchestrated the 1995 Tokyo subway sarin attacks. And it isn't just the extreme elements in religion. The ISHA Foundation, for example, has allegedly shown disregard for the law and environment. The Catholic Church has hosted various priests responsible for paedophilic sexual abuse of children, as they have admitted themselves. Faith protects its offenders blindly. In the end, religion is what allows holy men to commit unholy acts.

What Do We Do About Faith

So, does religion have a place in the future? To answer this question, we must first look to the past. Was faith required in the past? Did its benefits surpass its costs? Yes (at least until the 18th century). As Harari elaborated in *Sapiens: A Brief History of Humankind*, humanity could only reach these monumental heights due to its collective imagination and stories. Our society is merely our imagination and our social order and its conventions. Our most remarkable feat is not in their creation but in believing that these imaginations are real. But who am I to say they are not reality?

Religion was a cohesive force, binding humans together for the collective good. Its edicts on morality, livelihood and much else served as a critical story for the human mind. It inspired tribespeople to become large tribes, farm, create towns and cities and finally, whole civilisations encompassing the globe. Even the highs of science owe their existence to religion.

Science, The Child of Faith

The exponential expansion of science took place in many civilisations during different periods, usually in an isolated fashion. For example, in the 6th century BCE, the Indian subcontinent underwent a massive scientific, and technological transformation assisted dramatically by religion. Religion and science mixed freely, creating new hybrid philosophies. For example, Kanad's idea of the indivisible atom became a part of the Vaisheshika school of thought. Panini, the Sanskrit philologist and linguist from circa 6th century BCE, also founded the study of linguistics and the scientific theory of grammar, contributing to the Vedanga school of thought. Additionally, the magnum opus of ancient Indian medicine, the Sushruta Samhita, was added as a part of the Atharva-Veda and Ayurveda branch of Hindu scriptures after having discovered and successfully diagnosed and treated various diseases, including leprosy.

At the same time, the Hellenic culture was undergoing a similar expansion in science. Like in India, science began filling and expanding the cracks in Greek religion. The lack of religion led to the creation of the philosophical and scientific explosion centred around the tiny nation in the 6th century BCE and onwards. The Greek religion could not answer life's profound questions (which humans tend to ask), placing its philosophers, mathematicians and scientists on the job instead. So, from here, the world receives much of its foundation in philosophy and maths - the equations of Pythagoras, Thales and Euclid, the ideas of Heraclitus, Aristotle and Socrates, with the scientific contributions of Archimedes, Hippocrates and Galen.

Similarly, the African continent underwent a revolution under Greek influence post the 2nd century BCE. Egypt was critical to this scientific revolution, creating one of the world's largest libraries - the library of Alexandria. Africa was home to the Yoruba of present-day Zaire, who developed a range of impressive mathematics. There were even the Egyptians, who impressively estimated the value of pi to be 3.1605.

Genius was everywhere. How else can we explain the exceptional achievements of the Dogon people of present-day Mali in tracking various stars whose existence we have just observed (Sirius A, Sirius B)? These cultural exchanges between Greece, Mali and Egypt led to rich development in African philosophy with Ptahhotep, Ani, Khety and others. However, each of these discoveries had the element of faith.

Looking further through history past this classical period, we notice a similar pattern - the Chinese Scientific Revolution during the 10th century CE, followed closely by the Islamic Scientific Revolution and the Renaissance. Again, religion was central to the development of science. One could even say that religion was the parent of science, best when it was hands-off.

As Yoda says to Luke in the Last Jedi, 'We are what they grow beyond.' Science grew beyond religion, providing us with a globally cohesive and unified theory of life, connecting us far more than belief ever could. While faith lived, developed and died, science was eternal. After all, it was unchanging, lying just out of our reach. Science could have united us all. Yes, science has differences, but religion has divisions. Small wonder, science is the offspring of religion.

The Undead Zombies of Faith

How much ever we proclaim the death of religion, it always seems to come back and haunt us. It is starting to get annoying - the number of times we have to kill faith for logic only for it to come back more radical than ever. For a brief period, barely half a century, humanity has been on the cusp of a new scientific order without religion. And then, we were struck by a new wave of religious zealots. All of whom fed fuel to each other's fires.

Yet, what is the point of these old beliefs? How does religion fit into our world with the internet, nuclear weapons, and liberal ideals? How do Moses' commandments warning us not to kill stand with the need to protect citizens from inflicted duress? How does the sanctity of the

Ganges fit in with its most polluted vibe? When we began following these religions (the original faiths), they were not to spread so far and wide or encounter such novelties. Indeed, the sheer unpreparedness of the religious to face modernity was its end. I knowingly use the past tense - religion in its traditional sense is dead and dying.

Today, it certainly does not seem so. With the numerous religious idealists, terrorists and the new wave of political conservatism, it appears that religion has never had a better time in the past century. However, (let's hope) this is the last fight of faith, the swansong perhaps (if only ever so violent). With our generation having grown up accessing the most diverse source of information yet, there has been a cataclysmic shift in morals and ideas. Curtailed by the Millennials and Gen Z, religion as we know it has breathed its last. The only way religion can survive is to adapt. However, the central premise of religion in its know-all, see-all approach is the permanence of faith throughout time and space. Ill-suited to change, religion has lasted way too long.

No matter my morbid (to the religious out there) predictions, perhaps you feel that science does not have the answer to all of life's questions: that is true. Science has no replies. Yet it has all of them. Well, eventually, at least. Embodying Heroclitus's adage, 'The only constant is change', science accepts its fallibility and is willing to change. Unfortunately, religion cannot change - believers find solace in its static. When faced with adapting or dying, religion must choose between faith and propagation.

Still, there is considerable leeway for other forms of religion to propagate - freethinking, animism, deism and pantheism are relatively more adaptable forms of religion. Freethinking and animism being open to personal taste and far more interpretation (lacking scriptures) can change. Deistic religions believe in a non-interventionist creator, which is more accessible than other religions. Pantheistic religions, on the contrary, are mutable due to their deification of science. However, the greater freedom of thought proffered by these religions still raises an important question: does God exist? Does the society of the future have space for God?

God in Our Brave New World

However, what about the ideal society? Is there a place for God in our perfect society? Quite frankly, it does not matter. A person's personal belief in God is not a matter for any state to decide or try to influence. The problem with society is not the belief in God but its repercussions on ordinary people. The populace is usually attracted by the more cunning into various acts for some supposed God. This gullibility is not being able to differentiate between dangers and has hurt many people in the past. That is the difference between theism and religion. Theism lets people do stupid things alone, while religion lets people do stupid things together. The latter is deadly to society. Thus, more aptly put, the world of tomorrow has no religion.

The question of God has existed as long as religion. Nonetheless, the answer is a resounding no when it comes to the fore about whether God and religion matter to create a better world tomorrow. The world of tomorrow is built-in science and knowledge. The defects of the past with their forsaken eternity have no place in the future, as they remain to us only dead weights dragging us back. Though the task of convincing people to lose their predispositions about supernatural entities is difficult, it is not unachievable. We can accomplish this mammoth task with a combination of education, common sense and the normalisation of the question 'why'. Therefore, the book will turn from its relatively hands-off solutions to more of a guide for this venture. The idealist's guide to the ideal society awaits. It all begins with a sociomoral revolution.

PART VI

The tiny dragon was bewildered. But how could they question the intimidating dragon before them? What could they even say? So, they said one word. And that was enough. Just as the God-fearing dragon felt he had replied, our dragon would repeat his query - just one word. Soon, not even the fear of God kept the large dragon from acting out in denial. Here he was, realising that the bedrock of his life was not invincible. He couldn't believe how shallow he had been. And none of that would've happened without one word. 'Why'.

Why?

Or, Why ask Why

> *'The constant assertion of belief is an indication of fear'*
> *– Jiddu Krishnamurti*

The moment a child can talk, it begins to question. Most toddlers ask between one hundred to three hundred questions a day. How many questions do you ask? It's not your fault (you definitely cannot beat a toddler here). Since time immemorial, we have had issues with those who asked questions that were dangerous to our ideas. The Inquisitions of France, Spain and many other mediaeval kingdoms to the Mihna of the 9th century in the Middle East are testament to that. Even today, in our presumably freer society, asking questions about many matters is discouraged. Whether asking about someone's change in gender to the most trivial reason why they eat so much cheese, for instance, is seen on a scale of socially unacceptable.

One of the central tenets of idealism, the ACM, is based upon the ability to question and properly place new information. However, we cannot correctly debate a new piece of information unless we were to possess all the authenticated data. Thus, the idealist philosophy necessitates asking 'why' repeatedly. Curiosity killed the cat, but satisfaction brought it back.

Why We Can't Ask Why

Many reasons people do not support constant questions, as listed below.

1. They don't know the answer
2. They can't tell the answer

3. They don't want to see the answer
4. They can't doubt the solution, which questions will do

If a person does not know the answer, they often stray and dodge the questions instead of admitting their ignorance. Questions are like drills, digging deeper into the mind of the questioned until they reach the human ego. Nobody likes a shot at their pride. However, just like we should be fine asking constant questions, we should be okay not knowing the answer. Without accepting ignorance, we cannot have the bliss of learning together (for knowledge is always revelationary in some way).

If someone cannot tell the answer, they would dislike someone asking too many questions. But you cannot live in a reality of ignorance. Can you?

The Right to Ignorance

Often, people demand the right to ignorance - the right not to be made aware of the truth. Asking the right questions, as Socrates noted, had the effect of making people doubt their notions of the matter. Knowing this power, just like theistic philosophers avoid science, ordinary people prevent such questions, which may make them question their beliefs.

Otherwise, in some cases, people think they cannot afford to doubt their notions. They feel like questions will make them accept the facts, thus forcing them into cognitive dissonance. For example, a person who has devoted his entire life to praying to God doesn't want to know that his lord does not exist, thus refusing to answer.

However, that doesn't mean we can let them live in their reality of lies. We cannot let it slide when it harms our world as much as theirs. Just as the mighty dragon almost led a crusade against dragons, we end up damaging that which we value most in our blind ignorance.

Why Ask Why

The power of 'why' is fantastic; it can make people introspect without argument. A simple 'why' brings to fore previously unorganised thoughts.

Further questions only lead to a cognitive suspicion of hypocrisy. By creating dissonance in a person's mind, the right questions can win an argument on their own. Thus, tomorrow's society harnesses the power of the question. However, just as you must be ready to ask a question, you must be prepared to answer one. Indeed, conveying the clarity of thought at all points is paramount. It is alright to be unaware of an answer or unable to answer a question so long as you don't hem and haw your way out of it.

How do we normalise asking questions: by adopting the ACM and leading by example. First, we must begin to understand the power of the question: the information it provides and its effect on the person answering. The adoption of this social norm always starts small but conspicuously. Then, as explained in the chapter on idealism, they usually undergo a period of stasis until an explosion in followers. Hence, with patience, we can ensure that one day in our ideal society, people fully aware of the question 'why' will live, adhering to the philosophy of idealism and the ACM.

PART VII

The tiny dragon is now joined by a mighty, albeit tamed, ally. As they stretch across the skies, moving towards the giants, they leave a trail of fire. The lizards stepped through the curtain of blazes only to grow wings and follow the tiny dragon. The tiny dragon and their right-claw man, the mighty dragon, welcome all to their fold. Suddenly, the mighty dragon turns cold, his eyes as deadly as his poisonous talons. In front of flies a timid dragon with blue breath. 'No,' he proclaims. 'I know your kind and what they do,' he continued, ignorantly, 'You're a bluer. Get away! Get lost!' The tiny dragon is confused. What has this blue-breathed dragon done? Although she had done nothing, the mighty dragon could not bear to see one with blue breath in his fight against the giants. He felt they were not to be trusted. He just knew. The tiny dragon overruled him, but he knew that in the end he would be right. The tiny dragon could not fathom this hatred.

The Invincible Xenophobia

Or, How to Reduce Xenophobia

'What a sad era when it is easier to smash an atom than a prejudice.'

– Albert Einstein

Everyone has that one (or more) conservative relative who sits around commenting on the degradation of society with the new generations and their new ideas. They may be racist, misogynist, xenophobic, and offer unnecessary prejudices. Why? Why are we so prejudiced against those who do not resemble us? There are many theories - from the superficial to the sociobiological. However, one thing is clear: xenophobia has no place in future society.

The Science of Hate

The reasons for our prejudices are deep-rooted in our genetics, psychology and environment. We must hark back to the era of tribal man to find out why. Back then, humans often banded together in small groups called tribes. They were communal and close-knit, performing all critical activities together - eating, sleeping, hunting, having sex, rearing children and protecting. They had to secure the tribe not only from wild animals but also from alien humans and their foreign tribes. In the dog-eat-dog world of aeons past, trusting unknown people was exceptionally dangerous. Perhaps they would steal food, kill tribespeople, wreak havoc or spoil hunts. Depending on those who were not like us was a bad idea.

In addition, even if the foreigners were good, they could be carrying diseases they were immune to, which the tribe had not faced before - causing mass infection. That raises an important question: Does this not involve a lot of thinking? Why are we xenophobic for a bias so intrinsic to people today, without explicit instruction by their parents? As with humans, it's usually emotions first and logic next.

The reason? Reproduction. When two people procreate, their offspring has a genetic code amalgamated from his two parents. Thus, a baby looks like a mix of their parents without accounting for any genetic mutations. Therefore, a baby born to two Caucasian parents would likely have fair skin, just as a baby born to two African parents would have a flat nose. Back then, these differences were far more pronounced (with mating partners being few, to begin with). As procreation was strictly a tribal affair (noting the previous point of trust), racial differences became a part of our blood. We trusted those who looked like us because there was a higher chance they were a part of our tribe and would care for us as well.

That also led to negative feedback - we distrusted those who did not look like us. As love augmented the feelings of lust with our psychological evolution, this feeling grew in power. Love evolved for multiple reasons, one of which was the need to help keep both parents together to nurture their child. However, how could we procreate with those who were never present (with surety) and we did not trust? Thus, it was sensible to not have children with foreign tribespeople. As it so happens, our attraction to people is vital for human communication. So, love and tribal bonds gave way to a recognisable form of friendship (platonic attraction). Since we were not attracted to those who did not resemble us, we see the first form of xenophobia in history - racism. And that led to the second - war.

Casus Belli: the Human Version

War is an intentionally strong word to refer to the frequent raids between farming tribes. Often, hunter-gatherer tribes would join this complex game of raiding and war. Initially, it was because we needed resources - food, fuel, and such. However, as many generations passed, this grew beyond a game of resources. It became a primaeval version of Risk, the board game. With the complexity of war, the strong bonds of tribalism turned into patriotism. The second form of xenophobia is xenophobia itself (as we use the term).

Divine Intervention

The third kind of xenophobia evolved much later, beginning mildly in the circa 9000 BCE period. In the Fertile Crescent (one of the oldest neolithic civilisations - present-day Middle East), it is there that we see the first flickers of theism. However, it was not until the mid-2000 BCE that religion came about with religious scriptures such as the Pyramid Texts. Then came the many-gods Minoan civilisation, one of the first mythological epics (the Sumerian *Gilgamesh*), and finally, in the early 1000 BCE, the creation of the Rig Veda. The Rig Veda, the first religious scripture of Hinduism (previously Vedicism), was integral and marked a new era in religion: scriptures. From here, the Akkadian Gilgamesh, Akhenaten's monotheism, and the Upanishads all began. This history culminated in an explosion of faith from the 6th century - the start of the age of xenophobia.

Buddhism, Jainism, Zoroastrianism, Judaism, Confucianism, Taoism and many other religions resulted from this surge in theistic philosophy. Religion added a hazardous element to xenophobia. Now humans did not solely worry about resources, children and survival - they now had to care about a code, eternal hellfire and other divine consequences. Fuelled by the gullibility of the human mind and majorly the intrinsic motivators - genetics and environment - religious fervour captured the imagination of the common folk. It was not as much religion as the diversity of faith which caused the conflict. As various groups fought over the true God and the meaning of life, a new kind of xenophobia gripped people, which promised eternal torture and other consequences beyond a single lifetime.

Share of Respondents Who Answered 'People of Another Race' When Asked to Pick Groups They Would Not Want As Neighbours

Source: World Values Survey, 2014,2022

The Clash of Cultures

The fourth type of xenophobia to evolve was a culmination of all those before it: race/ethnicity, war and religion. It was cultural xenophobia. As society progressed, beginning to maintain complex trade contacts, many cultures came in acute contact with each other. Some hit it off with millennia-long relationships (E.g., the Arabs and Indians; the Chinese and Indians), while others did not (E.g., the English and Chinese; the Chinese and Japanese). To add on, there was logophobia (discrimination based on language). Even today, the inability to respect various cultures in certain people haunts society.

The Anti-Gay

Next arose the religion-spurred homophobia and transphobia. Finally, the fifth type of xenophobia was exclusively due to a lack of understanding of sex, gender and sexuality. However, certain societies did flourish as a counterfactual with pro-LGBT stances for aeons (India being most prominent). Thus, this exclusively religion-fuelled xenophobia was the next to capture the imagination of Christians, and Muslims alongside others like them, causing centuries of oppression.

'Darn Libs' to 'Pappu'

The sixth and last type to arise was political xenophobia. Today, in a politically charged world, all our previous biases have formed this monster — liberals versus conservatives, communists versus capitalists, aristocrats versus democrats. Arising from xenophobia, misogyny, and other issues, our stances often place us 'in the right'. This xenophobia is most widely accepted today, to my great dismay. From 'darn libs' to 'damn republicans', 'suit-boot ki sarkar' to 'Pappu', political xenophobia is at its zenith today. Even purportedly religious, cultural and xenophobic fronts are barely masked politics.

The Casting of Caste

A final footnote in the history of xenophobia is a particular case - caste. Regarding Hinduism, caste is a system invented in the first or second century CE (or at least written down by the Manusmriti). It consisted of 4 *varnas* subdivided into tens or hundreds of subsets called castes. We ranked each in an increasingly complex hierarchy - the top was called Brahmins, and those on the bottom were called Untouchables. Till today (2000 years later), this system pervades India, a unique form of xenophobia where members of a caste are scared of those in different castes. Indeed, it is recently that inter-caste marriages became prominent, let alone inter-faith. Religion and the human desire for social order spur another type of xenophobia: the religious type.

Types of Xenophobia

1. To sum up, xenophobia is of six types:
2. Race-based
3. Nationality and Ethnicity-based
4. Faith-based
5. Culture-based
6. Identity-based
7. Politics-based

- Special case: Caste-based

Caste Representation in Indian Cabinets Over Time

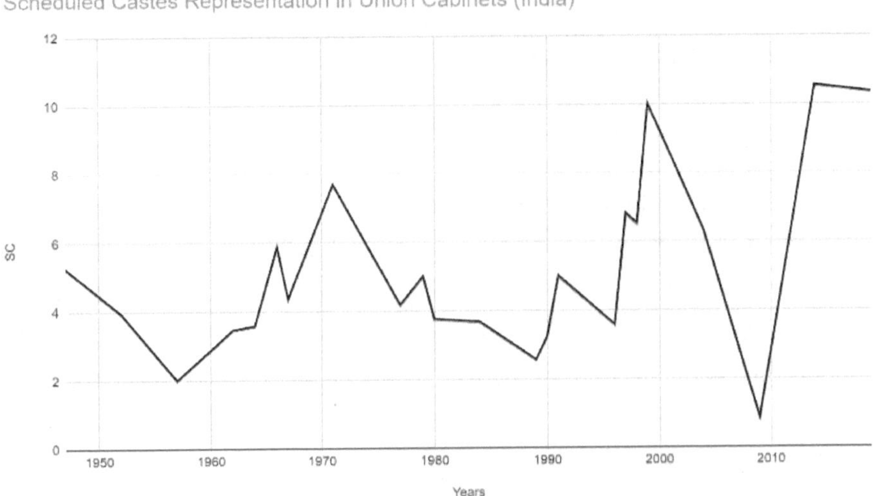

Source: Sneha Alexander and Prachi Srivastava, LiveMint, 5 Jun 2019

Tackling Xenophobia

Now, drunk with the past xenophobia, how do we sober up our future? First, we look at the root causes and work our way up. The problem with humans is their genetics and their environment. By altering both, as mentioned in the chapter on free will, we can achieve the most efficient solution to the xenophobia problem. But we can't modify our genes, can we? It's pretty impractical, even for me. So let's try something different. Let's take into account what we need to achieve and how.

1. A new system of education based on a human-centric view without national interests.
2. New future-based system of work to combat various problems, including xenophobia
3. Empowerment of a new method of organisation.

In other words, change must start from authority and education. Xenophobia is very intuitive and we must learn how to love diversity early on. While it may be too late for the mighty dragon in our heroic tale, it isn't too late for the newly-hatched lizards. Perhaps all we need to do is grow wings.

We will tackle the former two points in other chapters.

The International Loophole

The third point is of particular significance - a new type of organisation. Now, any organisation combatting xenophobia has got to be global. That is unless we want it to be a powerless figurehead. But in international law, we have a famous loophole. It's article 8 of the Montevideo Convention of 1933. 'No state has the right to intervene in the internal or external affairs of another.' Perhaps more precisely, this implies that any other state cannot intervene in everything that comes under a state's domestic jurisdiction. So, of course, that begs the question of 'what an internal affair is'. Anything happening in a country short of a war with another country seems like an internal matter. Even that can be considered an internal matter between two countries.

Now, there is a saving grace. Resolutions the UNSC passes are binding. However, that does not entirely solve the dilemma, for the UNSC is notorious for being unable to effectively resolve crises (pulled between various factions within it primarily due to the permanence of 5 members). Still, we must accept that those matters which affect a country internally affect the world too. Otherwise, why would a Syrian coup cause a worldwide proxy conflict or the murder of George Floyd cause a global outcry? Our world today is defined by its globalism, held back only by our xenophobia. Thus, there is a need to change our customs and laws for the harmony and progress of society.

Assuming for a moment that we could overstep this domestic jurisdiction, we would be able to create a council to prevent all xenophobia. That's the Consortium of Anti-Xenophobia Committees (the COAX committees).

Coaxing You Out of Xenophobia

Firstly, we must create a specific organisation free from government control in every nation to oversee xenophobia prevention. That's the COAX Committee. They would have a few responsibilities, like monitoring hate crimes and surveying people to understand the issue better. They'd then create and implement a national protocol to deal with the various types of xenophobia we discussed. And overall, they'd enforce international agreements on xenophobia.

To make things easier, we need to coordinate these movements globally. We'll call it the United Nations Office on Xenophobic Crime (UNOXC). This way, there would always be international support for COAX committees, even in hostile countries (which happens a lot). That would also help in administering justice in ICJ cases and protecting minorities.

1. Creating an autonomous semi-governmental body in every state (The COAX Committee) oversees xenophobia prevention in the nation.
2. They would be responsible for (in their nation):

    a. Monitoring all cases of legally xenophobic offences.
    b. Adding to the national censuses an additional column for xenophobic reporting by the people to better understand the demographics affected.

   c. Creating a nation-specific protocol to deal with offenders based on the six (or seven, in India) types of xenophobia.

   d. Ensuring that the nation's government falls in line with anti-xenophobia international law.

3. The creation of a UNHRC-UNODC office under the UNSC to deal with matters of xenophobia and control the network of COAX committees - The United Nations Office on Xenophobic Crime (UNOXC).

4. The UNOXC would be responsible for:

   a. Coordinating the system of COAX committees.

   b. Ensuring diversion of funds towards the COAX.

   c. Providing international authority to COAX interference.

   d. Collecting information with regards to Xenophobic crime by nation.

   e. Relaying important information for cases in the ICJ.

Naturally, for this protocol to work, we would require nine votes affirming the same in the UNSC to even introduce the topic as one for discussion. In addition, it would need four regular and five concurring votes (from France, the UK, China, USA and Russia) to pass again. Perhaps the proposal is too idealistic. Let us consider any alternative means of bringing about the proposal - amending the UN Charter. That requires ratification by 2/3rds of the world's parliaments, which is far more impractical. Why are these the only options?

For one, international law is *non-binding*. Ergo, no country has to follow any international resolution or law. They are only obliged to do so because it is 'the right thing to do'. Indeed, the fate of the world's progress rests on the want of nations to make sacrifices in the interest of the greater good. However, there are specific laws which are binding - conventions, treaties and UNSC resolutions. These, too, are only binding when ratified (the act of formally giving consent) by the country, which can retract this ratification if they deem fit.

Today, most of the essential conventions have received ratification from a significant proportion of the world (the UNCLOS 1982, the Geneva Convention 1949, the Montreal Protocol 1987, et cetera). If we were to achieve the same, we would have a chance to implement the COAX Protocol without the heavy hand of the UNSC in it (in a more democratic process). However, this is a complex process, noting that countries must secede a portion of their jurisdiction to an extranational authority for the COAX protocol to work. Left with this, we can only hope to compel nations to implement the COAX protocol themselves.

Institutionalised Xenophobia

But what would the COAX protocol do? Why would it prevent xenophobic crime? The protocol works to understand the domestic causes of xenophobia and find the most concise way of curing it. It is a transitory step between our current world and the idealist world. Most importantly, it aims to reduce institutionalised xenophobia.

Many countries today practise some form of institutionalised xenophobia. For example, almost every country practised identity xenophobia; many others practise faith and are politically biased. However, all forms of xenophobia are widespread, from mandated state religion to homophobic laws, dissent prevention to discrimination.

Imagine a system where a powerful extranational authority notes your policies and actions to raise cases against your country in the ICJ and your courts. There is no means of escape from the situation. That is the COAX protocol. It coerces states with legitimate international action (backed by the world's most potent committee) to prevent xenophobia. One could say it coaxes them into submission.

Xe-No-Phobia

How can an idealist stop xenophobia? Think, solve and support. Think about your beliefs. Have you ever thought (consciously or subliminally) of such thoughts? If you have, it is entirely natural. However, though defecating is biological, we don't do it everywhere; we have to control our genes. We have to hold what motivates us to think xenophobic thoughts. Refer to the ACM. Learn more about those who you seem to hate - it always results in a particular form of respect. To know who you hate is to know why you hate. Perhaps then you will see the lunacy of xenophobia and follow the ACM tactic to accept new information.

Idealists must not confine these revelations to themselves. There is a high chance that other people may be going to the same thoughts as you, which makes it all the more important to address. As you know what you have thought in the past, you know what they have supposed. Therefore, you must convince your peers to look beyond xenophobia. Indeed, this is not the final word on solving xenophobia, as there can always be better in the future. Thus, it is up to the idealists to innovate and implement these solutions.

Xenophobia has existed since the beginning of humanity and may continue to do so for centuries. However, the choice to veer away from its dangerous path is ours to make. Will we make the right decision or go down our current path of sure-shot ruin? The answer lies in the defining tasks of our life - our education and work.

PART VIII

Having settled debate on Xenophobia, the tiny dragon looked in front of him. There lay a giant. In its massive, hairy hands was a strange cage which imprisoned a dragon. This dragon was ten times the size of the largest dragon they had ever seen. If the tiny dragon freed him, they would gain a new and powerful ally. They sent a few red dragons to attack the giant. To their surprise, just as the giant moved to defend itself, the caged dragon roared and burnt the red dragons to crisps. She then glanced lovingly at her warden, the giant. The tiny dragon was disgusted - was this some sort of Stockholm Syndrome? After many failed attempts, the dragons realised that the only way to defeat the giant was with the help of a giant. Only then could they free the massive dragon from its caged romance.

Work ≠ Survival

Or, How the Future of Work Looks

'No one on his deathbed has ever said, "I wish had spent more time at the office."'

– Paul Tsongas

Work has always been an integral part of human life, despite its ever-changing nature. It gives us something to do in life. Some would say it gives our life purpose. I (having noted so in my chapter on the purpose of life) would differ. Work is the exertion done by a person to try and accomplish some task. To many people, work is the same as survival: a means of sustenance itself. It is the caged dragon of survival's giant. To others (the old rich, usually), work is laxer - a mere suggestion. However, for most of us, work is indistinguishable from a means of sustenance: that's how it has been for aeons (primarily because most of those people farmed for the food it provided).

The Drudgery of Modern Work

But today, work is (for most people) dull toil and struggle. Around 85% of the world's workforce hates their job. Why? The distinctly American philosophy of separating work from life in general often leads to this problem of monotony. Out of our usual 80 years of life, we spend about 40-45 years working and 20 years preparing to work. With such a massive impact on our lives, work should be something we enjoy and not merely a means to an end (basically, money to live). Of course, we often try to pretend it is - like the caged dragon pretends to love his imprisonment.

Only a very privileged few live in a world where they can enjoy their every day of work without worrying about survival.

In addition, another critical issue challenges work as we know it - Artificial Intelligence. As most readers would be aware, Artificial Intelligence is the ability of a machine/algorithm to perform tasks usually requiring higher levels of discernment and intelligence. It has become a giant in itself. The future is (to risk writing a cliched statement) AI. From transportation to hospitality, civic labour to even journalism, AI has become a raging inferno in the labour force. Or has it?

Thirdly, as ideas mentioned throughout the book become more viable, the very definition of work as necessary becomes incoherent. Is work essential? What counts as work if I can live with government support?

People Are Scared of AI

People are terrified of AI. Despite being the answer to all the questions in the last section, people fear that we'll become servants to the robotkind. To address all these questions, we must take them together. The future of work is not working as we know it, or even anything remotely similar. Quite a few people have speculated what work will be: often asking for more hype against AI or how AI will never truly replace human labour. All of these assurances are futile. Artificial Intelligence will inevitably take over your job.

Perhaps the capability is already present (it just isn't economically viable to replace you).

For context, if you are a journalist, there is already AI software replacing many of your colleagues every day. If you are a surgeon, there are already bots with the ability to perform more precise surgeries. Today, their scope is more limited. You use those tools in a symbiotic relationship. Yet, a human cannot learn from AI like AI learns from humans. The more you use these tools, the more precise they get. And one day, they won't be using you: they'll be perfect.

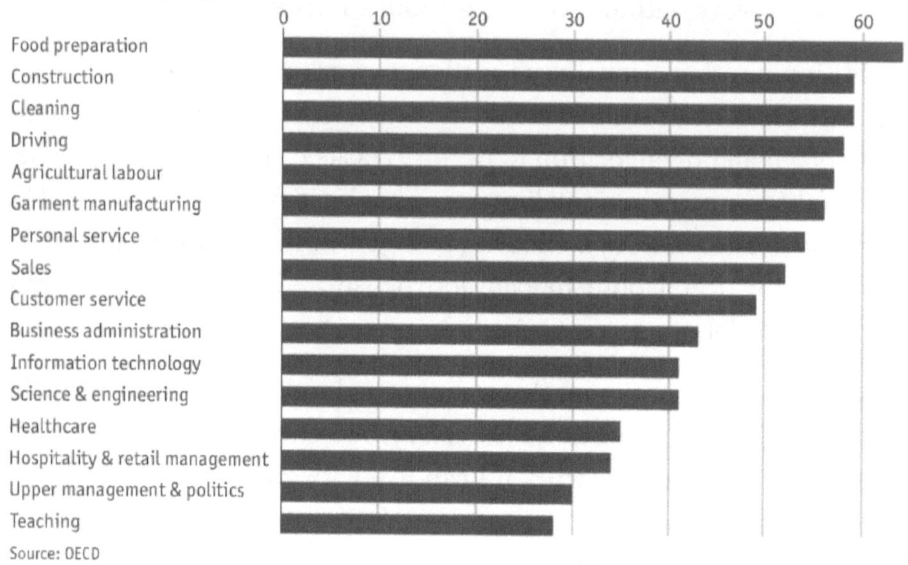

Source: The Economist

The previous paragraph, to most, would have presented a worrying situation. Within your lifetimes (of the average reader), you will probably see a monumental change in Artificial Intelligence. If you still work in 20-30 years, you may see your profession die out for humans, leaving you without a job. What do we do? For that, let's first look back at why we work and how it all came to be.

The Work of a Caveman

The purpose of our jobs is usually the successful completion of what our employers paid us to do. We perform these jobs to completion with varying degrees of success. At the end of achieving our jobs, our employers pay us the minimum they feel we deserve (or the minimum the government mandates). But there's a problem: we were not made for such work.

Once again, we have to look back to the primary bands of homo sapiens and our evolution as a species. What is the root source of the instinct to work? Probably the need to survive. In an unforgiving world where humans were constantly under duress from the environment and its constituents, humans evolved a need to do actions to protect their lives and communities. On the savannas and forests of Africa, we first learnt the need to work for a living. Back then, we had better work days - a few hours of hunting, some amount of tending to others in the tribe, et cetera. Our ancestors spent far less time at work than we do today. They also had rich rewards (vibrant food) and a good culture. Thus, we have always been able to work - but not as much as we do today.

r/Antiwork

Today, the average working hours worldwide are 9 am to 5 pm (8 hours), with the additional spillage of overtime. While the overall 10-or-so hours of work don't seem like much, our ancestors didn't do significantly as much. On the other hand, our ancestors also performed socially rewarding and helpful activities. Today's world is far more ambiguous. What social/real benefit can many of us see today due to us doing our jobs? That's a significant cause of employee dissatisfaction - a major driving force for a first-world phenomenon, the Great Resignation (2021).

As of the present, one of the largest online congregations of the anti-work movement exists on the popular Internet platform, Reddit, called r/antiwork. The trend raises an essential question about valuing the employee as much as the employer. In the one-sided relationship a worker engages in upon entering a company by caring for it, they end up tying themselves to a life of discontent. Unless we change the nature of work, nobody will want to (most people don't want to work where they are today anyway).

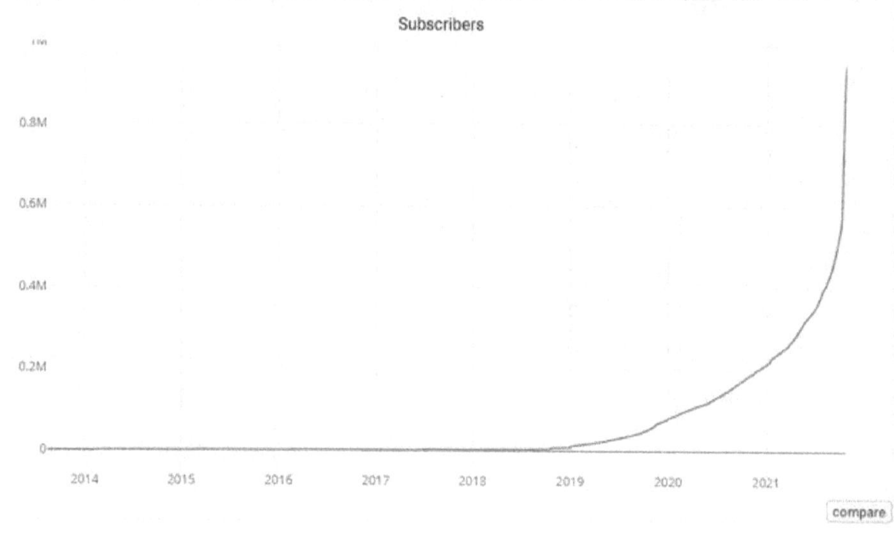

Source: Subreddit States, reddit.com/r/antiwork

Technological Death

So, what can we do, considering AI, motivation and the future? Accept it. We have to accept that Artificial Intelligence will take over every job we know today and those that will exist in the future. To protest the advance of technology and win is a neo-Luddite fever dream and impossible. In addition, this should be an outcome we should avoid at all costs. After all, that would imply shutting down technological growth and stagnating as a society. We cannot afford such an outcome considering the numerous problems humans must deal with today, of which AI is the only tool to help us. We cannot go into the future without shields protecting the general public from deprivation and a ready generation for the future. So, we must change our understanding of how we work and what work is.

Fields of work are like mortal beings - they live until their natural technological deaths. Be it the profession of the human alarm clocks or that of water carriers, they all have died due to technology (the mechanical alarm clock and the water pipeline). This law of technological death continues, a natural progression. Today's 'agent of death' is Artificial

Intelligence. We must congratulate ourselves on creating such an effective mechanism to end a profession. Tomorrow's work is based on the ending of occupations, bringing AI to every job. Be it law or coding, science or philosophy, AI signals the end to every niche.

Killing Our Careers?

How will jobs work? They will try to end human connections to a field as soon as possible. Thus, most positions will attempt to algorithmize the subjective parts of work. Then, perhaps, a cleaner theory of AI will emerge based on causal inference to delve deeper into more complex fields such as science and philosophy. We are turning the giants against one another to free the caged dragon.

What does this mean for the average person? A single person (in this time of change), as many future-oriented commentators have noted, may hold multiple jobs in their lives in various fields. However, unlike what most commentators believe, the sole point of their jobs would be to automate their jobs. Thus, a person working in a specific field would be aware they will inevitably be removed from their area by AI and have years to prepare for it. Indeed, they may move to a completely different field, aiming to relay technological death there. However, there is a catch. How can someone actively work towards the end of their career?

To us, it seems impractical. Work = Survival. However, Government-mandated basic living standards would make this unemployment exceptionally bearable - as is written in the following section. Work will no longer be the sole means of sustenance. This modern divergence of means of living and work will be fundamental to a sustainable idealist future.

Why Work at All?

But what about people who do not want to work? What about those who will live off solely the government's funds? Let them. In this world, it no longer matters whether someone is voluntarily unemployed (because they have sustenance and may not be productive either way in society). A person who is freely out of a job is probably best left without one - they aren't in the right state to commit to one. Government policies trying to make these voluntarily unemployed work will only result in half-hearted attempts to work and unsatisfying jobs with low productivity.

Another vital question to address is whether anyone would work. The answer is yes. After the modern divergence of work from means of sustenance, we would work because we want to. If you ask a small boy why he plays the piano, odds are he won't tell his desire to be a commercial pianist when he grows up. People often do things for no reason but joy: a further motivation is if it's suitable for the people involved.

That is why people endure so many scientific experiments willingly, put themselves at risk in a volunteering capacity and generally behave altruistically - it's their intrinsic personality. Indeed, once work diverges from sustenance, the number of hours worked will reduce - people would prefer to spend more time with their family and build better relationships. Perhaps, more will like dedicating their work to obscure but helpful fields which are less profitable. The benefits of such a divergence grossly outweigh any costs of reducing the number of hours worked. Naturally, the coming of AI would result in a lesser need for human time, who can spend their time elsewhere or for maintaining social connections.

The future of work is performing technological death. We, alongside AI, will be critical in increasing efficiency, productivity and potential in every industry - but only by killing its human portion. The road to complete automation of our jobs is long and will perhaps take a few centuries. However, a journey begins with a single step. It's time we grew confident in our abilities and took it. The future of work must come to the present. But how do we do that? How do we diverge work and sustenance? Via Unisism.

PART IX

The giant lay in a pool of his blood. The metal bars of the forbidden cage were smashed open. 'The giant is dead!' exclaimed the tiny dragon. A loud cheer ran through the ranks. They all sat perched on their new friend - the many-handed giant. She was a lonely giant who only rampaged forward. But, the death of one giant had only invited many others to come forward in vengeance. Many of them were adorned in strange necklaces and archaic rings. Some were two-headed while others had more. The tiny dragon let out a little flame of shock. His followers snarled, ready to go to battle. But they knew better than to fight: the lonely giant would not help them. They had to collaborate and weed out the worst giants. Perhaps not all giants were bad. Some were needed to keep the peace.

Unisism

Or, What is The Economics of Satisfaction

'The paradise of the rich is made out of the hell of the poor.'

– Victor Hugo

Imagine a person who wants to build a skyscraper. You'd need cement, glass, cranes, and so much more. Instead, this man has a lot of bricks and some superglue. Now, can he build a skyscraper? No. But this person is resilient - trying all possible ways to stack his bricks to make a skyscraper. It may look like he's making progress at times, but then the bricks all topple down because superglue isn't for such ludicrous ideas. That person is our economic system today.

Playing Jenga with Markets

Capitalism. That 'person' keeps trying to build skyscrapers out of bricks and glue. The rich, who benefit from Capitalism, shout to the person from encircling helicopters, shouting words of encouragement. They know and exploit the fact that there will never be a skyscraper. Ever so often, the rich veer too close to the tower of bricks, and it dangerously wobbles till it falls over—market failure. From recessions to depressions, there have been an increasing number of economic problems worldwide, many of which economists sweep under the carpet of 'the business cycle'. Every ten years or less, crises wreak havoc on global economies - and somehow, we've accepted this as usual and sustainable. How many times will the person sustain his bricks falling on him? One time? One hundred times? How many times until the person is unable to recover?

But why do these crises keep happening? There are a lot of theories, but as it happens, the main culprit is wealth inequality. It isn't the poor who have a stake in the stock market: it isn't the poor who decide their company valuations. However, the poor and the middle class bear the brunt of recessions. Not the rich.

Fixing What is Broken

The basic foundation of our modern socioeconomic system is wealth inequality. The gap between you and your neighbour is what drives today's system. That competition to earn the extra dollar and its compatriots are the bricks which build up Capitalism. Now, one could be dogmatic and extol the virtues of Capitalism yet know the wretched poverty that lies next to them due to that system's inabilities. Despite the myriad problems, many of you would turn up your arms and say, 'Capitalism is the best of the worst economic systems. We have no other choice!'

Many of you would think that pragmatically speaking (or writing, or thinking), Capitalism is the only practical economic system. This system asks us, 'don't fix what isn't broken' or laissez-faire. If you feel this is about fixing Capitalism, you will be mistaken. This chapter is about ending it.

Income Distribution (2010-2015): Richest 1% vs Other 99%

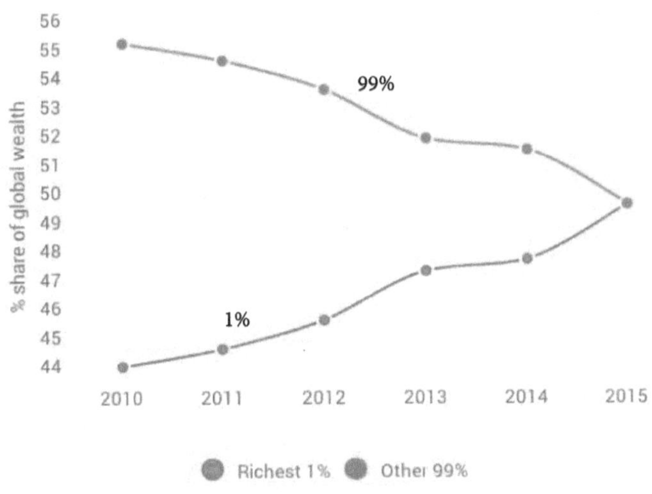

Source: The World Economic Forum

It is about the next economic system - the lightbulb to the candle, hopefully - Unisism.

Capitalism today is based on the following three major principles:

1. Selfishness is better and more efficient than altruism in its market outcomes.
2. Those who have wealth deserve it.
3. There is no alternative.

How Much Do the Rich Deserve?

Let's look at the 2nd principle. 'Those who have wealth deserve it.' This maxim is a fundamental principle of Capitalism, firmly founded in the concept of democracy. Capitalism arose during a time of revolution, where distinctions based on anything but merit were fast disappearing (at least for adult white males situated in Western Europe). Desperate for a new system of social structure, the revolutionaries looked inwards - most of the critical influencers of the victorious revolution were rich. And the usual way to get rich was trading - so they were merchants and businessmen. So, the system they adopted with great

The Business Cycle of the US: 1985-2019

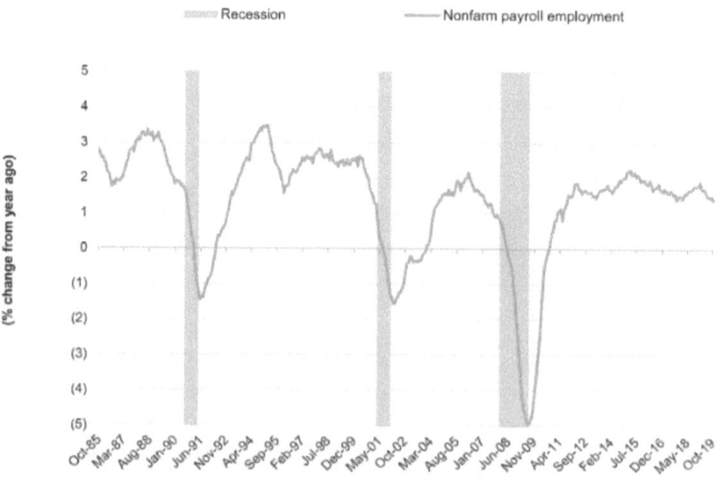

Source: Bureau of Labour Statistics

enthusiasm benefited their kind - Capitalism. Thus came the idea that wealth triumphed over everything - nobility, royalty, divinity, et cetera.

Mark Zuckerberg may not be His Highness, Duke of York, nor is the Archbishop of Canterbury. Still, he holds a higher social position than them - solely due to his wealth. Of course, some here would contend that it is not the wealth that places Zuckerberg on this pedestal but his innovation. However, there have been countless good ideas, better than Facebook (or *Meta*), such as Signal (for instance), which is non-profit (Of course, this is just an example). Thus, equating the wealth of an idea with wealth in terms of money is just absurd.

Additionally, what makes a person deserve millions of dollars per month compared to another earning just under 500 dollars. The work of a CEO may be necessary, but is it 300 times as important as that of a middle management employee? In addition, what of shareholders? A shareholder need not commit to even holding a job to earn millions of dollars on their shares. In other words, they make money by having money. And what of the critical political and social work figures of our lives? Where is their wealth? Nikola Tesla, Oscar Wilde, and so many others died, leaving us with the future and bereft of enough money.

Look at the world's poster boys of 'self-made' billionaires who grew up in 'capitalist' countries - Mark Zuckerberg, Bill Gates and Jeff Bezos, amongst others. Mark Zuckerberg went to one of the most expensive schools, tutored personally by a highly qualified software engineer. Bill Gates' mother was a high-profile board member at United Way: she was in close contact with IBM's then-chairman. That's how Microsoft got its first opportunity. Jeff Bezos was given more than a quarter-million dollars as a bailout by his wealthy parents to save Amazon. There is no 'self-made' in Capitalism. Although, as discussed in the previous chapter, all Capitalism calculates based on Equality of opportunity, there is none.

The Tautology of Greed

Let us look at the first principle: selfishness is inherently more efficient than altruism. Capitalists tell us that greed, inequality and cut-throat competition is the most efficient way to run the world. But, for some reason, it seems wrong. Communism tells us that proletarian dictatorship, revolution and socially equitable anarchy is the most efficient way to run the world. However, the base motives of the individual in either are the same - greed and selfishness. Why? All of these concepts come from the idea of the homo economicus (or economic man). It relies on the understanding of the perfectly rational consumer who maximises utility at minimum cost and work. As behavioural economists tell you, nothing could be further from the truth. Man is the perfect emotional consumer who uses logic not as a way to choose but as a way to justify his choice.

The basis of selfishness is rationality. The rational person chooses to be selfish. But who is a sensible person? Why does our society appear to work if we are not rational? It is because of what we see as people. Corporations are legal people. A corporation has neither personality nor emotion. Humans may staff them, but they are in their form, pure rationale. They are the ideal people who fit Smith and Marx's understanding of people's motivations. So, what is the proof that we are indeed not homo economicus? Could it not be that we are just confused and thus intrinsically selfish? To answer this question, we must connect the fields of evolutionary psychology, genetics and sociology. And we must look at babies.

Intrinsic Altruism

A baby below 18 months or so is closest to a blank slate. We prime for certain behaviours and are opposed to others. But are they intrinsically good? Well, as various studies show, yes. Not only do they exhibit known altruistic behaviour, but they also respond positively early on to altruism.

For example, an experiment in Kyoto showed 6-10 months old children three types of animations to decide whether understanding heroism (and thereby our sense of ethics and justice) is innate. One aggressive geometric character bullied and pushed down another character in all of them. In contrast, a third character watched from a distance.

1. In the first one, the third character escapes.
2. In the second one, the third character intervened accidentally and saved the second character.
3. Finally, the third character interfered deliberately and rescued the person in the third one.

The children had to choose a character (their favourite) in every animation. Who did they choose? In almost all cases, it was the intervening character. And, for ten months old, it was nearly always the intentional helping third character, as well. This experiment proved that we have an internal love for heroics and justice. We do not sympathise with the selfish escapee, nor do we sympathise with the narcissistic bully. The one ideal we strive for as humans and understand is altruism.

Some of you would say that this behaviour is limited to ideals, which need not be correct. But does this extend to places where optimising utility comes into play? Again, yes. A study from 2011 shows us that, even when referring to universally loved gummy bears or beautiful stickers, humans act altruistically. A lot of three-year-olds were taken and divided into teams of two. Then, the researchers showed each group a transparent box with four treats trapped inside. The box had one or two holes through which children could access the treats, but to access them, they had to work together to pull a curtain rope. Now, this led to a dilemma. If both children worked on the string, would they share the treats when one took them? Yes. Now, when the box had two holes, both children could get the goodies equally. But, when the box had one spot, the child who took out all the four treats would share the first two passively with his teammate. Unlike modern society, it would seem that anger and altercations were virtually not present. Man is born a saint, but civilisation makes him a sinner.

Now that we agree that we are born selfless, we can discard the myth of homo economicus. However, in the absence of a better alternative (as the third principle goes), we must choose Capitalism. Thankfully we do have an option: Unisism.

What is Unisism?

Unisism is a socioeconomic theory, an idea to unite the classes of society via market forces. So, what is the motivation of Unisism? The goal of Unisism is to merge all previous socioeconomic classes into a single entity through market forces and government policy, thereby eliminating class distinctions in the long run. It is a lofty goal, seeing the wealth inequality in our society. It may sound unfeasible, but it is essential to our community, as I show you below.

But before that lies the fundamental question: why merge the classes? What does that even mean? Firstly, in our modern-day society, as Trotsky and Marx noted, we have five classes (albeit Marx mentioned two): The bourgeoisie, the petty-bourgeoisie, the salariat, the proletariat and the lumpenproletariat. We don't need to remember that. Either way, their meanings in today's society slightly differ from their 19th-century counterparts. Here is a table to clarify their intentions:

Class [Top to Bottom]	Description	Example
The Bourgeoisie (The Exploiters)	The highest class who are usually paid not in traditional means, with most (if not all) income from exploitation of labour (via stocks or such).	CEOs, Venture Capitalists, Influencers, Certain celebrities, et cetera

Class [Top to Bottom]	Description	Example
The Petty-bourgeoisie (The Stooges)	Consists of professions who may make it to the highest class, often engaged in labour involving overseeing multiple people while paid in a mix of traditional and non-traditional means.	Upper-level managers, Celebrities, Influencers, Successful politician, et cetera
The Salariat (The In-betweens)	Consists of professions where people are paid monthly/annually (a salary) involving retribution for labour/ services offered.	Scientists, Government officials, Middle/Lower corporate employees, Researchers, Teachers, et cetera.
The Proletariat (The Exploited)	Often considered the bottom class, consisting of blue-collar workers, wage and contractual workers.	Plumbers, Factory workers, Cab drivers, Deliverymen, Sweepers, et cetera.
The Lumpenproletariat (The Destitute)	The lowest class, consisting of the inadequately self-employed, frequently unemployed and underemployed.	Small farmers, Unemployed, et cetera.

Thus, we have the Exploiters, Stooges, In-betweens, Exploited and Destitute. However, Capitalism tells us that it is crucial to have these distinctions for society to function efficiently. The chasm of wealth inequality is supposed to motivate all the other classes to earn money and 'act rationally'. Clearly, without a disgusting celebrity with an extensive criminal record, there is no way we would be motivated to achieve more!? And it's perfectly alright for the elite to splurge wealth in the name of 'investment'. The main economic reason behind this is often called the Trickle-Down Effect.

Down the Hole It Goes

Imagine that you have a lot of wine glasses stacked on top of each other like a pyramid (like you see at the Ritz or those fine-dining restaurants). Now, pop a bottle of champagne and let the alcohol flow from the bottle onto the single topmost wine glass. What happens? As any physics student would inform you, the wine flows into the glass, fills and pours down into the subsequent glasses beneath it and so forth. Economists (precisely the capitalist thinkers) use this analogy to explain the need for wealth inequality. They believe that the rich must remain rich and untaxed so that they may spread their champagne - money - to the poorer, who continue the chain till the end. But unfortunately, this is never how society pans out.

The bitter truth comes in the form of orthodox Marxist theory. Imagine a bottomless thin pit with a funnel. And you're pouring your wine into it, for some reason. Occasionally, a few drops spill on the sides. But they immediately slide off into the pit because it's a funnel.

This wine wastage is the state of the economy. The poor often appear to receive money as paychecks and salaries, but they can never use it! I quote the *Communist Manifesto* - '*No sooner is the exploitation of the labourer by the manufacturer, so far, at an end, that he receives his wages in cash, that he is set upon by the other portions of the bourgeoisie, the landlord, the shopkeeper, the pawnbroker, etc.*' The wages they earn are grabbed away by other economic agents for sustenance. They, too, are not free from these obligations. Only one class is genuinely free from these obligations - the modern bourgeoisie. Thus, just as they receive their freeing wine, they are forced to give it away, and so forth until the top class receives it. And there it sticks and is enjoyed.

This 'Wine Wastage Effect' is quite logical and common-sensical. More than 40% of the world lives under $5.50/day. With that sort of money, one can hardly get through the day - having to spend on a minimum of 2 meals, commute, utilities and such. Perhaps if they saved a dollar a day and lived this frugal lifestyle, they would get about 3 dollars per week. How long would it take to save 1 million dollars? Six thousand four hundred ten years and four months. That's about 80 average human lifetimes. Perhaps that's unfair. Let's imagine he saves his money in a bank with an average real interest rate of 2%. That dramatically reduced the time required to 246 years, or more than three average human lifetimes. To save up the income Alice Walton gets in an hour. And she inherited her wealth (She is the heiress to Sam Walton, founder of Walmart). How does someone get so rich while others stay so poor? Capitalism.

The Wiles of Communism

But communism is not much better. The communist theory relies on impractical anarchy of the state. But what about our natural calling to order? Such a gross power vacuum gets filled, often unwantedly. Humans always revert to order and hierarchy - they are, after all, social animals. Thus, Marxism is very limited in its post-revolutionary scope. That is because the need to organise is critical to human progress - it has significantly contributed to technological and economic progress over history.

The idea of forcing socialism down the throats of the rich is an appalling precedent. What's to say that these classes will not form again anyway? This question leads us to Leon Trotsky's theory of Permanent Revolution - that revolution must keep taking place to prevent the entrenching of bourgeois government control. However, the costs of rebellion are high - think about the costs of a constant revolution! Perhaps we should look at Lenin, Stalin, Mao, Kim Il-Sung or Prachanda. However, they all lack democratic values, both in politics and economics. So, there is some truth to the statements made by economic think tanks about the futility of communism in its vicious cycle of revolution and dictatorship.

'The history of all hitherto existing society is the history of class struggles. Freeman and slave, patrician and plebeian, lord and serf, guild-master and journeyman, in a word, oppressor and oppressed, stood in constant opposition to one another, carried on

an uninterrupted, now hidden, now open fight, a fight that each time ended, either in a revolutionary reconstitution of society at large, or in the common ruin of the contending classes.'

Thus, we need a new, more efficient strategy to tackle problems than just beginning another bloody revolution or intrigue. What is the answer: efficiency and cooperation. Perhaps it is not willing cooperation, but it is better than hacking off heads and stealing wallets. We need to homogenise the classes. In other words, we need Unisism.

The Ideas of Unisism

Capitalist economic thinkers often use this opportunity-outcome dichotomy to explain the superiority of Capitalism in terms of income. It would be unjust to prevent citizens from earning more than their peers directly in our future society. But we can't constrain people to one income class either - that would be economic suicide! To live up to an individual's maximum productivity and economic potential, they must be free from additional burdens that do not plague others. Is it fair that they remain poor just because someone was born in a low-income family? Perhaps it is student debt or mortality tax; these generational accumulations fetter their ability to earn an income. People should be free to earn an income in any way they choose from the initial accessible starting point. But how do we get that starting point?

The Economics of Satisfaction

Firstly, we must begin by changing the moral motivations of society. That might sound implausible, but remember that governments have been doing this for centuries. Those taxes and subsidies have all been to push you in specific directions. This time, we're changing society more dramatically. However, the framework for implementation remains constant.

Secondly, we must change our goal from searching for welfare or profit to satisfaction. Our economies appear to progress for progress' sake. Many developing economies pump dollars into their economies to inflate their egos and statistics. How much does that help anyway? People do not want to have more. They want to have more than someone. It is not greed alone that fuels the market. The poor compete for survival, the middle class for jealousy and the rich for greed. And we have to address everyone, not only the rich (Like Capitalism does).

Thus, we have three main objectives in the economics of satisfaction:

1. Provide basic survival needs.
2. Equalise and harmonise classes to remove disparities.
3. Convert greed into a socially optimal virtue.

Basic Amenities Provision

Today's world requires a host of amenities which provide a platform for progress - an equal opportunity for everyone to thrive. What are these basic human necessities which the government must provide? As you'd expect:

1. Food and Drinking Water
2. Health and Hygiene
3. Security
4. Education
5. Internet
6. Transportation
7. Electricity and Gas
8. Retirement care
9. Capital

Food and Water

The first and most important is food and drinking water - a fundamental right of people. The idea that a person does not deserve water/food because they don't have money is a mindset we cannot propagate into the future. Besides, why are you against someone else getting food and water? To be unable to afford, access or find food is food insecurity - a massive worldwide problem. However, most governments today provide some assistance to ensure a supply of clean drinking water and proper local food. Yet, some governments do not provide this basic human necessity as a right (most importantly), most famously, the United States of America (and Eswatini and Singapore, amongst others).

Health and Hygiene

Secondly is the right to health and hygiene. The right to access affordable healthcare services and practise proper hygiene is fundamental to the development and maintenance of any society. This right includes the government providing (at the least) primary healthcare - ICU, ambulance, health check-ups, generic healthcare drugs, birth control, menstrual products and their disposal, hormone-boosters, essential therapy, proper medical counselling, and minimum health insurance, amongst many others. It is just as critical to include psychological issues and gender dysphoria in the right to healthcare.

Security

The third is the right to security for a person. A person must believe that he is safe in his home and workplace. This security is paramount to a prosperous economy - which must be a positive-sum game for humanity to progress. Armies usually help us here alongside police forces and (in some regions) private militias. Unfortunately, while most of today's world is subject to the direct consequences of man's action, tomorrow's world will fear the indirect consequences - climate change and resource depletion. When the water rises, will the police forces follow old Emperor Caligula of Rome, who declared war on Poseidon and stabbed the seas? While helpful today (debatably so), in tomorrow's chaos, we face outmatched forces. We must ensure the provision of security against man-directed crises and man-created ones.

Education

The fourth is the right to education. Horrifyingly, many countries do not possess a strictly implemented law providing all students aged 14 and below with proper education for free. The economic gains are practically boundless - we could see the next Einstein rise from the slums or even the next Pele! Imagine the number of immensely talented children wasted due to their inability to find proper education by competent teachers. Most countries today provide some form of free schooling to students. Sadly, most of these free schools are not well-equipped or efficiently delivered. These public schools are unfit places to learn with unpaid staff and lack essentials such as textbooks. Meanwhile, students from the top 1% go to elite private schools worldwide, with one-on-one tuition and a plethora of features such as international field trips, famous mentors, and professional assistance. How do we ensure this new policy of education? Compulsory and free education till 18 is essential (and optional, but highly subsidised college education is also paramount).

Internet

Fifth is the right to the internet. Many experts often view the right to the internet as impractical - requiring smartphones, and which poor man has a smartphone? Surely governments can't provide billions of smartphones? These would have been valid arguments had they not been factually inaccurate: most of the world has smartphones and rudimentary internet access (around 80%). The world of tomorrow is on the internet. To prevent someone from accessing the internet because they are poor prevents them from becoming more prosperous. Most major social media/internet companies came to be around 2010. How many of the world's top 5 under-25 wealthiest entrepreneurs owe their money to this platform? Every single one. Thus, the right to access the internet is akin to the right to a future.

Transport

Sixth is transportation. The lack of safe, secure, usable transport is often detrimental to a society's development. Many cannot take jobs far from their homes without sacrificing their families for work due to the lack of transportation. People (especially women) often cannot work night shifts/late because their transport is unsafe (between work and home). This issue is a severe economic disadvantage and productivity sinkhole.

Electricity and Gas

Next is the right to electricity and gas. That is an obvious requirement for a living - without electricity or gas, one cannot cook or sustain themselves. To put it dramatically, one cannot live properly without electricity or gas.

Retirement Care

Penultimately, we need government-funded retirement care. Post-retirement, a person should not have to work for a living. After working for 30-40 years of one's life, a person has earned their respite. The elderly should not be straining themselves (unless they want to) to live. After funding the government for so long, it is the government's turn to return the favour and care for them.

Capital

Finally, the government should provide capital (however, we shall cover this in the next section of the chapter). That may seem insane at first. How do we provide such a comprehensive programme of social benefits? Primarily, we have to understand that most countries already offer (at least a portion of) these goods.

In Conclusion

Food, water, health, security, education, and utilities are often already provided in most developed countries (barring the US: they're scared of being seen as 'socialist' or 'communist' or, worst of all, 'Marxist'). The remainder - Internet, retirement care and transportation - can be provided by utilising the below-mentioned policies. Specifically, the happiness tax would drastically increase tax revenue for countries. A person earning 100 million dollars in annual income at a reasonable 60% tax rate barring the happiness limit would give about 59 million dollars in tax.

In addition, by forcing corporate reform, we could force ISPs, Banks and Transportation companies to provide free transport (unless the government can give them already. By redistributing funds from various schemes providing other reliefs mainly due to a person's poverty and excluding plans involving a person's marginalisation in society (temporarily), we can also budget funds for this Basic Amenities Provision Project. But what's all this sudden change? Let's start from the beginning. What is the Happiness Tax.

The Happiness Tax

Today, there are three major taxation systems - progressive, proportional and regressive. Progressive taxation systems increase the tax rate provided to a person with an increase in income. That means the tax amount they pay is positively exponential. We can see this system in countries like Sweden, Belgium and Denmark. Proportional taxation systems have the same tax rate throughout, so the tax revenue increases linearly with income level. This taxation is visible in countries such as Mongolia, Russia and Kazakhstan. Regressive taxation systems have decreasing tax rates with growing income. That means that the tax amount they pay is negatively exponential. Such systems are visible in many countries as the VAT and Sales Tax. How do we ensure Equality of outcome in taxation?

As explained in the chapter on Equality, money buys you happiness to a specific limit. For Americans, that's a minimum salary of $75,000 p.a. (according to Credit Suisse) Or $37.5/hour (for an average 8-hour workday). However, it isn't solely the ability to earn 75,000 right now that matters, but the ability to do so in the next few years (say five years).

So, we utilise the average salary and wage rises per year to demarcate a salary which will eventually rise to $75,000 over a decade. There aren't any reliable statistics available for this figure but assuming that the yearly rise for individuals under 50 is x% at a given salary S, their salary in 10 years would be S(1+x)10. When S(1+x)10 = H (H is the Happiness Limit), we can say that S is the Tax point (in a progressive society).

At a 4% increase in income p.a., the annual salary should be $50,670 initially. That is about $26/hour.

For taxation, the concept of Equality must be one outcome, for the tax must have the same effect on everyone. Thus, a person earning $26/hour should be taxed. In contrast, those earning below two-thirds of this should have zero, if not negative, income tax (not random). This system would account for the data, including taxation accounting for the happiness-wealth correlation. That's about $17/hour. The rudimentary formulae:

1. S = Income; x = Rise in Income/year; H = Happiness Limit; n = Years accounted for
2. $ST = H(1+x)-n$ [Tax point for achievable happiness]
3. $SZ = 0.67ST = 0.67H(1+x)-n$ [Zero/Negative Tax point for happiness]

Social Inheritance

Inheritance laws. In today's world, individuals usually divide their assets via 'wills', distributed post their death. Usually, we pass on these assets to family, friends and charity. Thus, Elon Musk's children will have a considerable head start with their income, education, amenities, and much more. So that means there is no longer a similar starting line for Elon Musk's children and another middle-aged Pretorian civic official from the same high school. So how do we solve this problem?

Modern society lies on the relay of inequality. While the rich/powerful get richer/more powerful, the poor/weak get poorer/weaker. After all, it is a consequence of the Wine-Wastage Effect. Most economists refer to this as the vicious cycle of poverty. Poverty entails not only a lack of money but an inability to afford many essential amenities of life - education, utilities, food, financials, internet, et cetera. As mentioned in the chapter on Equality, there is a significant discrepancy between a poor woman's son and a rich woman's son due to the differences in their upbringing facilitated by wealth. How do we break this chain of ill?

Not by providing money and schemes - this is a change in the very mindset of society. Thus, we must understand that it requires a monumental shift in our values to curb the current problem of poverty and any such pain in the future. We must not punish a child for his father's sins. The answer: socialising inheritance laws.

Take a relatively well-off person who passes away, leaving assets worth $500,000 in his sole possession. Ordinarily, he would have created a will to determine how to split these possessions to whoever he deems fit. Leaving that for now, take another poor, debt-ridden man who passes away. His total assets amount to nothing - his liabilities, however, are worth $100,000. Ordinarily, depending on various complex laws regarding inheritance, these liabilities are passed on to their spouse or children. Imagine being set back $100,000 without having good enough employment either way. That would perpetuate the cycle of poverty previously mentioned. Therefore, I propose a (notably radical) policy. Half of all assets and liabilities (set apart expressly in one's last will) will be transferred to the government and distributed amongst society. Let's look at the maths behind this, with the US as our case study. There are 1,027 deaths per 100,000. Imagining that the number of people dying reflects (over time) the wealth distribution nationwide, 10% of people have 77.1% of annual income in the US.

This sum amounts to (accounting for the retirement of an average of 20 years, 35 years of work with average income and 40% savings compounded over time at a real interest rate of 1%) $270,433,645 for those 102.7 rich deaths. In other words, an average of $2,705 per person per year. To put this in context, this is about 22% of Andrew Yang's famous freedom dividend (UBI). The actual value of this social inheritance would naturally fluctuate (even the average would be different because this is only for the top 10%). However, we must also calculate for paying for half the liabilities of a dead American - it's the society's fault just as much as it is theirs for also letting. That amounts to (on an average) $46,451,210 per 100,000 living people to pay. That's still $223,982,435 or $2,240 per person (19% of Yang's freedom dividend). That said, I realise the capacity of humans to misuse laws creatively. Thus, to reduce such misuse, here are some clarifications:

1. If they wish, people may decide to split their wealth in a way they deem fit between society and their heirs. If the valuation of these assets is equal to that left to his heirs in the present and foreseeable future, they will be honoured.

2. Upon procuring the death certificate, the probate court or national equivalent will direct the division of assets based on valuation experts and the will of the deceased.

3. Large transactions (as per national standards) made in the month preceding the death of the person in question (especially to family and friends) will be considered inheritance and accounted for in settling the will.

4. Similarly, debts undertaken in the quarter preceding the person's death do not warrant consideration. However, this is subject to change in the relevant judicial body.

Unisist Corporations

The capitalist corporation is a front for unlimited greed, exploitation and societal devastation. From the most fashionable and hip ones to the old boring snobbish ones, almost every company today is capitalist. From Apple to Pfizer, Reliance to Softbank, every company you buy from is capitalist. Now, in itself, the capitalist corporation is not bad/wrong. It is a good idea, I concur. An enterprise catering to supply and demand with routine technological innovation? Hell yes. However, in practice, it is pretty destructive (the bitter opposite). Why is it rare to find a celebrity involved in slavery/forced labour (E.g., Allison Mack) but easy to find a corporation engaged in one (E.g., Apple, Nike, Disney, [although it is not the same kind] et cetera)? And why is it that while celebrities must repent for the rest of their lives, companies need not?

The answer is Capitalism. Self-interest makes companies do strange things for profit, even enslaving people for their work. There have been multitudes of controversies (well-publicised and investigated). However, we continue to use these products, fully aware of what the companies have done. Why? Because we cannot live without them. The larger a company, the longer it lives. What would you expect of a company utilising harsh sweatshop labour, child labour, illegal practices of tax evasion, corruption, et cetera? If you desire any action, you would be woefully mistaken.

Today's world is supposedly governed by 'democracy'. Democracy is the concept that every man has the right to decide the government's policy. However, hypocritically, to represent yourself, you need to have access to more than adequate wealth or some such patron. In other words, only the rich have representation in a modern democracy (although it often looks like the poor are true). This horrifying dependence on the benevolence of the rich is the most sickening trend of today's world. And who's richer than companies? Thus, our world is not truly (in the real sense) democratic: it is plutocratic. How do we solve this crisis? We have to reinvent corporations themselves.

Let us call these new corporations USCs (Unisist Corporations) and the old ones CVCs (Conventional Corporations). A USC does not care for conventional goals such as profit, sales, stock prices, et cetera. Instead, they work towards a far more profoundly impactful goal: social welfare. Many of you will immediately disagree and dismiss a world made of USCs. After all, where is the drive to innovate? Or the financing? Let us compare the CVC and USC markets to answer the first question. In a CVC market, corporations routinely stifle innovation when there is a conflict between innovation and revenue (the problem of profit). Ever since the last century and a half, when Capitalism was said to emerge in its current form, we have seen hundreds of instances of the problem of profit. Famously, there is the story of the eternal lightbulb.

The longest-running lightbulb is the Centennial Light bulb at a Fire Station in Livermore, California, USA, which has been lit almost continuously for 120 years since 1901 (about a million hours).

Our most innovative commercial light bulb - the LED - has an average life expectancy of 50,000 hours. The incandescent light bulb (which the Centennial Light bulb is) has an average lifespan of 2,000 hours. What happened? Capitalism. In the early 1900s, various of the world's major light bulb manufacturers - TEPCO, Phillips, Osram, et cetera - decided to limit their products' abilities to continue selling more light bulbs. At the time, the height of light bulb lifespans was about 2,500-3,000 hours which fell to just 1,000 hours.

The Light Bulb Conspiracy: The Phoebus Cartel

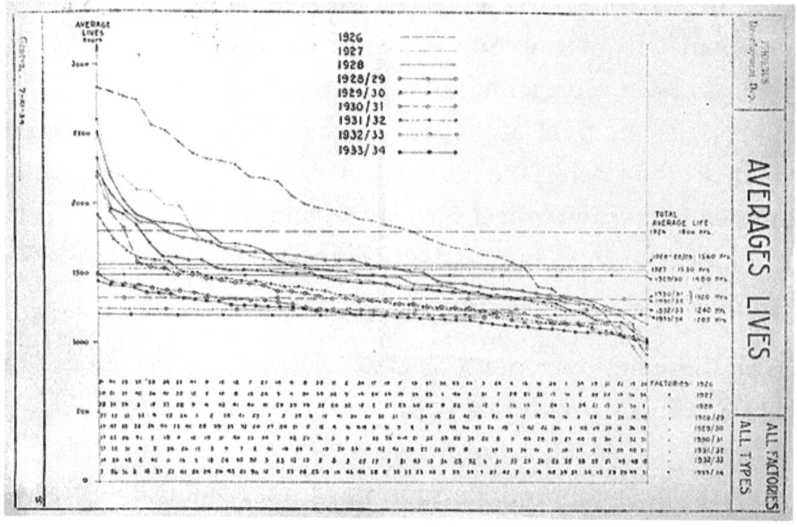

Source: IEEE Spectrum

Similarly, Eastman Kodak, the developer of the original Polaroid camera, calculatedly prevented innovation from keeping their core business - selling film for cameras. So naturally, when digital cameras came to the market, Kodak went out of business, running aground quickly. However, the prototype for the digital camera was Steve Sasson's idea from 1975, who worked for Kodak! Not wanting to disrupt their steady market, Kodak kept this discovery under the wraps, being their bane eventually. Perhaps thousands of such instances are happening the moment you read this book, yet none of us is aware yet (as these corporations have not failed). Capitalism often touts the need for creative destruction, yet Capitalism itself delays and prevents it from taking place.

Now, in the USC market, there is no motive to hide a discovery from the world. On the contrary, cooperation for social welfare would be the norm. The market is motivated by an urge to contribute to society itself, and innovation is the most significant way to do so. So, we come to the question: is social welfare a strong enough motivation? Yes. As explained in the last chapter, the future of work depends on the divergence of work from sustenance. Thus, a company built around such work, provided the prior two policies are in place at least, could ensure a thriving conducive environment for a USC. After all, with the purpose of work being technological death, a USC is just more logical. It would have no reason to hold back further progress as we see CVCs doing. But how does a USC market function? Since USCs work on social welfare, investment is difficult to find. There are only two willing sources of investment - donations and government funds. With the lack of funding, the obvious way to get resources is to sell company control.

However, a USC cannot remain socially motivated if a board of directors hijacks its power with their motivations for the company. As donations are rare and unpredictable, we find a single funding source: the government. We come to another critical question: isn't this just government control? No. As explained earlier, everyone has a particular list of rights to be provided by the government, one of which is the right to access capital. Thus, serious business proposals aiming to further social welfare should receive capital funding from an independent source. An entity governed by permanent rules with no further government intervention - like an Electoral Committee - would be set up, possibly termed the Capital Access Requirement Management Association or CARMA.

CARMA go through a person's proposal and their records regarding criminal history and then provide government funding based on the project and its idea for five years. After that, the government would fund CARMA utilising increased taxation. As USC markets set in, providing more of the market than governments, the increased strain on the government's treasury to support various programmes and capital requirements will decrease too. The USC market will thus provide for the people. In addition, the idea of taxation for USCs is no longer as potent since the lines between NGOs and USCs get blurred further on. Thus, soon there would be 0% USC corporate taxation as they try to increase social welfare. However, these tax benefits come at the cost of shouldering responsibility and accountability, making USCs the face of Unisism.

As much as we must try and work towards such a future, it would not be easy to come about in less than a decade. Thus, we would make specific transitory changes. CVCs must be made transparent, innovation-friendly and socially beneficial in their activities. In addition, it is vital to increase regulations and penalties regarding corporate tax evasion, environmental and labour protections, and corporate-government funding links.

The last point is exceptionally moot in a 'democracy'. I'll discuss that in the following section on the future of governance. None of this is viable without international cooperation - opacity, laxity, and bribery abound in chaos (which the global system regarding corporate regulation is in). There are very few unanimous laws regarding corporate law worldwide (enforced by a spaghetti bowl of Free Trade Agreements, multilateral treaties and bilateral agreements of varying levels of legality). Thus, without further emphasis on international standard norms in business, we will continue to live in a world where nations race to the bottom. And for what? To attract MNCs for pompously puffed-up statistics such as GDP, selling their resources and people for generations of exploitation.

Indeed, to set these norms is to prevent this new-age corporate slavery (which is still every bit as racist as it once was). The days of sweatshop labour and exploitative contracts will soon end, facing technological death. Yet, CVCs hold us back, preferring 'cheap' human labour with thousands of negative externalities to 'expensive' automated work.

Via international norms, increased domestic regulation and a revamping of what is considered corporate, we can change the corporate world as it is today into a market of USCs. It's time for a regulatory revolution.

Conclusion

Unisism is a theory based on changing perceptions of human behaviour in economics and modernity. It is an inevitable product of the catastrophes and cataclysms we undergo due to our people - from environmental disasters to genocide. As a result, the world is in dire need of a way forward and unity. Yet, Unisism alone will not be enough. Its implementation depends on an alternate political system (not democracy)— a webocracy.

PART X

Now, the dragons were not merely dragons. They were saviours and bringers of peace. The tiny dragon discussed the future of their ruined world with the amicable giants. But how would the world work - the dragons were many but the giants were powerful. What sort of alliance could they strike? Not an oligarchy, said the dragons. Not a democracy, said the giants. The problem was not power or numbers: it was equality. How could the two species be equal? The tiny dragon thought long and hard. However, there seemed to be no escape from this fundamental dilemma. Until, that is, they heard the mighty dragon berating the blue-breathed by meddling in their affairs (again). One of his victims bit back. 'You don't get to insult us,' said the brave dragon, 'We've suffered this discrimination enough. You have no say in what we do!' Could this be their path to peace?

Parsamanity

Or, How to Reach Equality Through Inequality

'To those accustomed to privilege, equality feels like oppression.'
– Ruth Bader Ginsburg

Equality is tyrannical. Now, before you cancel me, you should hear me out. This chapter is not about devaluing anyone's opinions - it's about giving them more of a voice. To all of you, the best way to value someone's opinion is to understand that they are equal to you. But how? In what way are you comparable to them? Certainly not genetically. Let's say genetics is the basis of equality. Chimpanzees share 99% of their genes with us (we share 0.99% more with other humans). Does that make us equal to chimpanzees, too, allowing them access to voting and legal recourse? No. Though they require rights, voting is not one we give a chimpanzee because their opinion (if they could understand) about a human problem like abortion is irrelevant. And frankly, they don't care whether we get abortions or not. Sadly, we can't say the same about the human race (we do love to meddle in the affairs of others).

The Origin of Equality

Now, how did the idea of equality come about if we weren't even biologically similar? From religion. Almost every religion tells us something like 'all souls are equal (in judgement) to God'. Then they add phrases implying that believers get preference and your sins weigh against you, et cetera. But, taking only the first portion about everyone being equal before God, liberal thinkers came up with the idea that everyone is equal. In a period of constant discrimination and disarray, this was admirable and brave. But, despite their noble sentiments, equality was doomed to fail from the beginning.

I could write about how nobody tries to achieve equality, but the problem is not that. We have a long way to go to achieve equality in gender, sexuality, minority rights, et cetera. The issue is when we achieve perfect equality - when everyone is equal to each other in terms of political representation and before the law.

The Tyranny of Equality

At the root of equality is the seed of inequality. Only by making everyone equal do we consign ourselves to the flames of our world. So, let's split equality into politics and law. Politically speaking, why do we want equality? Because we want our opinions to be worth just as much as someone else. But why? Imagine you are a 22-year-old fertile woman carrying a child for whom you cannot provide. However, you can't get an abortion because of a strange 55-year-old infertile man living on the other side of the country. His choice voted out yours, although his life is relatively unaffected (compared to you) whether or not you have an abortion. And we are talking in terms of physical and economic bases. Is that fair? No! Why is someone utterly unaffected by a policy still having the same value as you in making that decision. In other words, why is an unruffled majority getting to decide the fate of a minority? This problem of majoritarianism (both by numbers and power) is rooted in the idea of political equality.

Similarly, let's look at equality before the law. Imagine you and Jeff Bezos were on the same highway, driving considerably above the speed limit. You get caught by the traffic police, and they fine you a hefty $1,000 (Rs 75,000). Now, who do you think this affects more? You. $1,000 is a lot of money for you, although it may not be to Bezos. But that amount is like pennies to Bezos. So, although we committed the same crime, Bezos gets away without a scratch on his life while you may drown in backlogs of payments. However, everyone is equal before the law, so everyone faces the same punishment. Again, imagine you and your notorious neighbourhood politician have committed the same theft. However, who will walk free with lesser repercussions to their lives (because with political charisma comes a fan following)? Not you.

The Idea of Parsamanity

So how do we fix this? Is equality an outdated concept? Or can we build upon the original idea of equality and change it to fit the future? The idea may feel wrong to you, accustomed to equality. However, the alternative to equality is not inequality. It's the equality of outcome taken out of its usual context of income. As I like to call it, it's not equality before the law but equality by impact. Or, as I would have it known, Parsamanity - beyond equality.

Usually, when we discuss equality, there are two schools of equality - opportunity and outcome. Imagine that humanity is in a race. Then, everyone begins on the same starting line according to equality of opportunity. But equality of outcome says that everyone should finish on the same line. We often think of the two as immutable and utterly distinct. Lamentably, we are thinking about it all wrong. Let's stop considering the present and instead consider the future- Parsamanity. How does an event affect a person in the long run? In essence, the idea of Parsamanity stems from a single sentence - what if we had equality of impact? Then, every stakeholder has a vote with a value depicting the amount it would affect their lives (without considering any base effects that affect them all). So how do we implement this idea?

Progressive Punishment

We've talked about how rich people get to avoid the law's full impact because they are rich. I hope you agree that it is not fair since the whole point of the law is to ensure that they punish a person for their crime. And being poor isn't a crime. But, fear not! There's a simple and elegant solution to ensure Parsamanity before the law. A person's punishment should be proportional to their income and power for any crime. Most of you would be appalled by such a suggestion as it appears to remove the perceived equality we possess. For example, if you fine an individual Rs 10,000, their life would be affected dramatically depending on their income. Perhaps a high-income doctor can afford it, but a street hawker cannot. In addition, we must also take into account their families. Maybe they are the only earning members of their families. In this case, imprisoning the sole breadwinner is problematic because it leaves a family bereft of income.

So, how does Parsamanity want us to solve this problem? First, make the law like a tax system - progressive. The richer you are (in terms of net worth), the more punishment you get for your crime. And it's not just the amount of money that increases, but its proportion compared to your net worth. Just because 10% of a person's income is a lot for the poor doesn't mean it's the same for a billionaire (he still has $900 million of a net worth left). In essence, progressive punishment would ensure the same impact on a person's life for every law. Perhaps then people would begin to understand the need to stop jailing people and start rehabilitating them too.

Equality by Section

Now, we can see an obvious problem in implementing Parsamanity in politics. How can we equate a policy's impact on stakeholders if we elect representatives? These MPs and Senators have the same problem - they cannot represent everyone however much they try. Therefore, they cannot tell you how the women in their region would vote for an abortion policy. Who can? The woman. But democracy is highly inefficient as a system for implementing Parsamanity. So, I've come up with an alternative to democracy: the Webocracy.

PART XI

'Then it is settled!' exclaimed the self-proclaimed head of the giants. The tiny dragon's new system had been accepted with much gusto by both parties. But how could it ever be implemented? Out of the blue, the landscape went silent. The dragons and giants looked around, flummoxed. There was a periodic dull thudding - but that was all. All of sudden, a large roar echoed through the ruins. A massive creature with the head of an alligator, the body of a lion, the wings of a dragon, and the tail of venomous serpents emerged. From afar it had seemed like a giant dragon. 'No!' shouted the tiny dragon. But there was no escaping fact. This creature stood in between them and their peace. Whatever it was, it could not be allowed to exist with them.

Webocracy

Or, How to Govern Through the Web

> *'Power is everywhere; not because it embraces everything, but because it comes from everywhere.'*
>
> *– Michel Foucault*

Democracy, by far, has been one of the world's oldest and most successful forms of governance. Being a great idea, it caught on with many nations across the globe. From the societies of hunter-gatherers to the Indians and Mesopotamians of the 6th century to the Greek founders of democracy just decades later, democracy has continuously evolved to fit the times. It was usually a direct system, consisting only of 'free men' or elders in its initial form. A bit ironic, considering that democracy was supposed to be governed by the people. I guess that's what happens when you aren't considered a person. Soon, democracy came to encompass a right to political representation, freedom, and Equality under Pericles and Thucydides (basically aged Greek men). And then, suddenly, democracy as we know it was born in Rome with their SPQR or parliament (indirect democracy). But Rome was a one-off experiment in the classical world. Democracy is an inherently unstable form of government. Such experiments happened again - but to no avail. It's challenging to be the only democracy worldwide because nobody else has to care about popular opinion and elections like you do. Still, humans are very attached to ideas, and we persevered.

And this determination paid off: what we had hoped for arrived. The United States of America declared independence from the British. It went on to form one of the oldest surviving democracies. After this, countries begin falling to modern democracy like dominoes (though very slowly at first). The ripples of the American Revolution travel across the world, contributing to the 1789 French Revolution, the 1791 Haitian Revolution, et cetera. Then, in the 1840s, various European nations faced democratic revolutions, majorly due to the 1848 Revolution of France. Soon, modern democracy ceased to remain a majorly Occidental phenomenon, with Persian democracy from 1905 and further decolonisation resulting in various independent nations throughout the 20th century. In the end, the Romans did conquer the world.

We Aren't Ready for the Internet

Two thousand years later, what has changed? True, we have laws, Equality and rights, but is democracy made for today's times? Sure, it adapts, but will democracy alone save us? Did it save us the last time the whole world faced a threat? Perhaps it is an illusion which we cannot help but accept, just like our dragon's face. The people critical to developing our idea of democracy lived at least two hundred years.

No one saw the Internet coming (but that's what change is: disruptive). Nikola Tesla was the first to scientifically foresee this, imagining a wireless data transmission system and working on a theory to support it. Until 1925, scientific opinion about such a system never existed. Until the 1950s, the scientific community did not take it seriously either. And political thinkers weren't focusing on these breakthroughs in communication technology anyway. So, when the Internet came, governance continued as usual. A lot has changed since the 1980s, but nothing has changed in the most critical ways. Is democracy the way into the future for our world?

Many of you may point to systems like plutocracies and monarchies. And sure, we could debate many other forms of political governance (monarchy, theocracy, technocracy, et cetera). Yet, the world's most pervasive and sought-after political system is democracy in the modern world. And yes, democracy is the most inclusive and representative of them. But if you've read this book well till now, you know that if we don't change ourselves, others will change us. And when they do, we won't have an option to save ourselves.

The Downfall of Democracy

You may ask, what's wrong with democracy? You probably know the answer - it blares at you from newspaper headlines and shouts to you from your government offices. Still, let's revise the many problems people have with democracy - its fatal flaws.

1. **Political instability** - Governments have very short lifespans in a democracy - often leading to alternate extremes coming to power. These shifts change focus from critical issues plaguing a nation to the rally of inconsequential power moves. Like the snakes of the monster's tail, politicians attack each other, aimlessly spreading venom.

2. **Representation** - People often cannot represent themselves, becoming instruments various political parties use for power. They cannot express in their entirety who they are. Although the monster possesses the wings of a dragon, it is nothing like a dragon.

3. **Ignorance and Jargon** - We are usually unaware of our parliament's laws. Even if we know, we can't read them easily. We know their power - we can see the teeth of the alligator. But we cannot see their snouts and how long the leash of the law goes.

4. **Political Equality** (which we discussed in the chapter on Equality) Yes, it is the lion in the body of a monster. Unfortunately, its addition to democracy only makes matters worse.

5. **Corruption** - The inefficiencies of bureaucracies haunt every democracy in the world. But this flaw forces us to pay the expense of these issues ourselves. Corruption is the mind of this monster. Democracy is a monster which follows money and power mindlessly, much to lament of the people.

So, how do we solve this grave crisis of affairs? We turn to the innovation of the millennium - the Internet.

The Age of the Internet?

Think about it. If we are, when did this age begin? Many of you will say that the age of the Internet started around twenty years ago - after Sir Tim Berners-Lee created the World Wide Web. An exceptionally west-centric view. In 2000, about 500 million people had access to the Internet (less than eight per cent of the world's population then).

Today, more than 4.6 billion people worldwide have access to the Internet. That's about 60% of the world! As we reach a state of ~100% Internet access, we already see a world where everyone knows everyone. With the advent of hybrid realities such as the Metaverse, the age of the Internet has just dawned on humanity as we begin to realise its full potential. The age of the Internet has just begun. But the Internet is just a tool. Just as we can use knives to chop vegetables or kill people, we can use the Internet for many (sometimes questionable) purposes. And so, we come to the defining question of our time: how does governance apply when we have the Internet? The answer: rule by the Internet. You're probably thinking, 'What' or 'Ok, why'. Let's see why.

Cultural Blurring

Through the Internet, a man in Wichita, USA, can buy sweet potatoes from a self-owned business in Lae, Papua New Guinea, entirely without government supervision, using cryptocurrency. It's amazing! Moreover, the two undertaking the transaction will probably never even know each other. Yet we understand each other so easily: because there is more similarity than difference between us. And we keep growing closer together as humans. The Internet has brought us closer together, blurring what constitutes a culture.

Today, many Gen Z children possess similar interests and have similar references and cultures regardless of nation. A Pakistani boy and an Indian girl can get along nicely while playing some popular game like Valorant with no problems, talking about their favourite subreddits. Most people do not recognise this remarkable milestone in human history. Never (never) before have different cultures understood each other more than today. We've gotten so used to the Internet we've forgotten life without it. When was the last time you visited the library to research your project? Life without the Internet is unfathomable, especially for people my age and younger, born with phones in their hands. The Internet is a machine of creative destruction. The Internet destroying thousands of regional cultures has created a new digital culture. This blurring of cultural lines is an essential component of the future. We have to consider its impacts on the idea of a nation. You're probably confused: how does cultural blurring affect a nation anyway? Well, in every way possible.

Modern states consist of vast territories, often with many ethnic variations. Nevertheless, these variations often blend into a single national identity, brought about by some common struggle or past. Take India, for example - it consists of more than two thousand ethnic groups. However, it's a single nation due to its unifying struggle against the British. Then there are nation-states, countries usually consisting of a single ethnicity /social group. They, too, are unified by a common struggle and their shared culture. As a result, each country has its specific culture or set of cultures, unique from other countries (more or less).

Today that is fast becoming untrue. Despite various accusations of 'cultural appropriation' and such, the world will continue to assimilate in culture. The rich, poor, Chinese, American, male and female communicate on the Internet. They do not require English knowledge: we can instantly translate on the Internet. How do we continue to manage a country where men and women identify more with people worldwide than their next-door neighbours? What is the need for a nation if we possess no shared identity? If our children, regardless of where we are in the world, share the same culture, what makes every nation different? Nothing. It's a hard truth to learn, but culture is the base of any country. If nothing makes us different, there is no point in other nations. In that context, I introduce you to the idea of the World Wide Webocracy.

What is the Webocracy?

The World Wide Webocracy is the hypothetical government of the entire world governed by the Internet. As I like to call it, it's a 'cyberstate'. A cyberstate, unlike a modern state or a nation-state, is a state which exists only on the Internet. It does not require land, only a population whose location doesn't matter (to the Webocracy). However, suppose we were to broaden the idea of what territory is to include Internet space. In that case, a cyberstate is just like any other state today. It has people, government and land. It just does not have borders. However hard you try; the Internet cannot be divided along country lines. There are no immigrants on the Internet because the Internet is home to everyone. That's the idea of the Webocracy.

Disclaimer: The Webocracy does not mean we no longer have physical nations – it is only the governing aspects of the world which handed to the people. There are still physical jobs and people, as you might have guessed.

The Principle of Webocracy: Everyone deserves a life on the Internet.

The Life We Deserve

So, what is this life? First, you probably want to know what I think are the basic requirements of life. So, let's start from the basics: our rights. In the Webocracy, there are ten fundamental rights every citizen possesses.

1. Right to life.
2. Right to free expression.
3. Right to belief.
4. Right to free association.
5. Right to protest.
6. Right to dignity.

7.   Right against exploitation.
8.   Right to the Internet.
9.   Right to privacy.
10.   Right to legal process.

Right to Life, Free Expression, Belief, Free Association and Protest

The first five are obvious, general rights that most of the world is supposed to have already. They tell us that we have a right to our bodies (Life), minds (Expression), emotions (Belief) and actions (Free Association and Protest). But, of course, they come with exceptions due to criminal activity on their part (hate speech, criminal groups, et cetera). These rights tell us that the Webocracy must protect its citizens regardless of their beliefs and associations and cannot harm their bodies and minds for protected actions.

Right to Dignity and against Exploitation

Right to dignity implies that every citizen deserves a life of dignity, free from discrimination, abuse and deprivation. Adding on to the freedom parade, the right against exploitation vows to prevent citizens from exploitation (organ or sex trafficking, bonded labour, et cetera) which is standard on the dark web. These rights ensure that such atrocities do not mar a person's life on the Internet.

Right to privacy and the Internet

The Right to the Internet informs us that we cannot deprive a citizen of access to the Internet. So, it makes perfect sense, right? Imagine that the government suddenly shut you inside your house with your windows blocked and doors locked. You can't go anywhere or see anything. You would know nothing about the outside world except what you feel. You wouldn't meet family and friends. Is that fair? No. That's what access to the Internet is for a citizen of a cyberstate.

But accessing the Internet usually comes with a lot of caveats. For example, how do you ensure that your private data, whatever you do on the Internet, is kept confidential? Activists have taken many giant tech companies to court over privacy concerns (E.g., Meta, Google, Amazon, et cetera). And if that isn't enough, governments worldwide invade our privacy too! Mass surveillance has become a rising threat. The world's classified agencies do it - from the RAW to the Mossad, NSA to ISI. It doesn't matter if you have nothing to hide. That someone can seize all your information and social media and even view what you're doing in life should frighten you. The Webocracy, inheriting this hidden dystopia, will have to protect its citizens' privacy, even from itself.

Right to Legal Process

However, none of this is possible without efficient and functioning courts to defend the rights of citizens. So, just like in any other democracy, we have a judicial system. And everyone can access it at any time - even if they are convicted of a crime.

Protesting Online

We're all accustomed to roadblocks, sit-ins, picketing, marches and vigils, et cetera (physical protests). But, as times evolve, so should our methods of protesting. That said, in an Internet-centred world, protesting online has its fair share of advantages:

1. **Accessible.** The Internet is open to everyone - including for protests. Political issues don't matter to a computer - your activity is in the form of objective code.
2. **No geographic restrictions.** People are not restricted by where they live or whether they can arrive at a protest - it is online.
3. **No loss of life.** Offline protests can often turn violent because of the police, protestors, or counter-protestors. Online protests don't try people's tempers like that - so it's a win for everyone.
4. **Quicker.** As the protest is online, it takes a relatively shorter time to peak — you can see why just below.

5. **Reaches a wider audience.** The Web is worldwide, so every protest is worldwide (some more than others), making people aware of everyone's plight.

6. **Cannot be ignored.** Just as we cannot overlook roadblocks and sit-ins, we cannot ignore DDOS attacks and cybervandalism.

And that last sentence is controversial. For those of you who have not set foot in the troubled waters of online protest, people have debated the legality of these actions for quite a long time. You've probably noted the massive surge in hacktivist attacks (surely, you've heard of the Anonymous, LulzSec or the Legion of Doom). And many people ask whether hacking or defacing websites is a legal way to protest. In a Webocracy, things go two ways. Hacking is illegal, but some of these alternatives would probably be good ideas to implement:

1. **Distributed Denial of Service Attacks.** A distributed denial of service attack (for the non-programmers reading this) is an attempt to burden a website with fake traffic that actual users can't access the website. As of when I write this, governments have essentially criminalised DDOS attacks. Even as an alternative to sit-ins, they are said to 'infringe' upon private property, i.e., the website. The most important reason is the economic loss suffered by the website (obviously). However, regarding protecting free speech, citizens will be allowed to carry out limited DDOS attacks (to prevent their usage by cybercriminals) with a permit from the policing algorithm. In addition, involuntarily compromising computers to use them for performing a DDOS attack will continue to be strictly illegal (involuntary botnets). See? Everyone's happy. Except maybe the website against which they're protesting.

2. **E-petitions.** These are pretty standard today. Most people have seen or signed at least one of these unless they live in a digital cave.

3. **Email lobbying.** Mostly legal, even today, if you can legally obtain email addresses. I wouldn't say that this is controversial, so.

4. **Social media/Hashtag activism.** Everyone has seen this. You go to Twitter's Trending tab, and you see this. Of course, it's not always impactful, yet it spreads awareness.

The Quest for Governance

But how do we protect and enforce these rights? Furthermore, how does the Webocracy get anything done? Two ways: automation and population. The Webocracy automates the processes of taxation, licensing, social services, cyber police et cetera. In other words, the general day-to-day activities of the government are automated. Now, you might say that's too far out. Perhaps you're saying we don't have the technology to create these tools.

However, there are precedents to each of these. For example, there's a good chance that the income taxes you pay are already the output of some computer programme, and their collection is automated. And cyber-police AI has already been tried out and may already be used. In June 2021, Cyberpol created DIABLO 616, a cybercrime-fighting AI. And in September 2021, the Chennai Police Department announced a similar lab fuelled by AI to find cybercriminals. So, we have an honourable line to say that the bureaucracy of governance - the executive branch (as your country may call it) - can be automated.

You may say that that's alright for the executive, but what about the judiciary? As it so happens, we are already automating judges. Many cases in China, specifically corporate ones, are already being decided by AI. In addition, AI assistants can increasingly support judges in deciding criminal and civil cases. So, an automated judiciary is already a reality. But, of course, we cannot rely purely on algorithms in such delicate matters, so we would have to let people appeal severe cases to a human panel. Even then, a highly digitised judiciary would ensure total obeisance to the rights of every citizen.

How to Be Political

So, that leaves a huge question. How does politics work in the Webocracy? With the help of everyone. Imagine a platform, perhaps similar to Reddit. But instead of their everyday thoughts or memes, citizens submit proposals, specifying details in an easy-to-read language about their plan. As you all might know, you see Reddit posts by scrolling down, with the top posts having the most upvotes and the lowest ones having the least.

In the same way, the public can 'upvote' or 'downvote' a proposal to move it up or down the proposal ladder. We would tie the website to the citizen's virtual accounts; impersonation and spamming the ranking would be improbable. But, remember our chapter on Equality? We should be politically equal in the long run, based on the impact policies have on us. Thus, our votes are not equal on every topic. So, while proposing, a person will rank a few identifiers, giving people with different identities different values for their vote, even on the proposal ladder. People would discuss the policy and suggest changes on the platform as well. Depending on the proposal's popularity, it would reach the top of the ladder.

On a designated date every month, internet users, divided regionally (Each unit will consist of approximately 1,000 people), would read the proposals in the order of the proposal ladder and finish voting on as many policies as possible. So, depending on how pressing people think an issue is, it gets voted. Eventually, every submission will have debate unless public opinion is drastically against a particular policy. Those meetings will be all about discussion, implementation and governance. When the users have completed this, every citizen will be allowed to vote either 'yes', 'no' or 'abstain'. Amended policy proposals can be submitted as new ones for public review again. Then, the platform would combine the results worldwide (or regionally, depending on the proposal's scope) and declare them. If an absolute majority by value passes the law, it becomes a law. If it fails, a person may submit a proposition multiple times - public opinion changes over time. But say we succeed. There's no government to implement these laws. Or so it seems.

There is - but not the way you think. Suppose you've just convinced the world of the need for a policy. You will then nominate ten other members to form a 'government' for implementing the proposal. Of course, just because you proposed something doesn't mean you have the time to implement it. Fear not! You can nominate someone in your position too. Still, you're not doing this for free. Each member will receive a general salary for their assistance.

Suppose your policy's government fails to implement their proposal to the general public's expectations. In that case, any citizen can raise a recommendation to cancel the project. We must note that these governments cannot use resources apart from those they specified they required - and can only govern about their policy. After implementation, the council may meet periodically to review the regulation. At the same time, the government should work towards automating the task (as mentioned in the chapter on Work). An administrative programmer working for the policy government will accompany the committee for this task.

The To-Do List

So, what does the Webocracy want to achieve? And how will it ensure we do reach it? Many issues come with taking care of a global cyberstate.

1. How do we protect citizens from cyber conflict?
2. How do we ensure that our data servers (for holding citizen information and critical web infrastructure) are physically safe?
3. How do we provide for our citizens' physical needs - food, shelter, life, et cetera?
4. How do we secure the Internet as a part of the Webocracy?
5. How do we ensure everyone has access to the Internet?

Some of these questions have relatively simple answers, as many of you probably figured out. So maybe we need an army of counter-hackers or cybersecurity experts. Or we need to hire people to guard the physical data servers of the Webocracy. However, how citizens answer these questions will decide the course of the Webocracy.

Why Webocracy?

Time for the reasons. Why would we willingly leave our current world for this Webocracy? After all, I agree that our present world is improving, though not the best.

There are Six Main Problems with most governments today. And our cyberstate solves each one of them - to the benefit of every person.

1. Political instability
2. Centralisation
3. Representation
4. Ignorance and Jargon
5. Political Equality (which we discussed in the chapter on Equality)
6. Corruption

The Statistically Stable Government

People have extreme opinions. Societies do not. Because if we all accept a stance, it isn't radical anymore (by definition). Yet, we continue to elect people to power, not societies (or groups of people). So, we have an apparent reason when we complain about how democracies keep oscillating between extremes like a pendulum. People are constantly changing (often overnight). Societies are stable: they take time to change. Sure, things can spur them into action: that's what we idealists count on to change the world. However, we want a world where people can still change the world without sacrificing its political stability.

As you might have noted, the Webocracy excels at this. Based on the idea that people can decide for themselves and voice their opinions, it tells us the voice of society. Thus, we see that change is simultaneously accessible and challenging. People have an easy way to change the world while simultaneously needing to make it understood by society at large.

So, statistically speaking, the Webocracy would be a government which truly can make people happy. The only way to convince the world about something is via discussion and compromise—the way a democracy is *supposed* to function. We are truly creating a world where change is possible. The Webocracy is an opportunity to beat social inertia, finally.

Power to the People, Finally

The radical decentralisation of the Webocracy is significant to understand. For the first time, the idea of democracy can be more than a promise. Unless you belong to the 6.4% of the world that lives in a full democracy, you know your democracy is flawed. It isn't what we expected it would be - not because people didn't want it, but because it isn't feasible. Not with a democracy. The Webocracy offers us a chance out of the graveyard of hope we have dug for ourselves.

As you may have noted, there are no politicians in the Webocracy, only leaders. Therefore, every citizen who wishes to change the world can. There are no restraints or barriers which will affect us anymore. If this is not continuing the lore of democracy, what is?

The End of the Political Compass

The Webocracy is the end of the political compass. Parties, left-wing, right-wing and such labels no longer matter. Political affiliations steadily lose meaning - as political parties have no motivation to form. We do not need politicians anymore. There is no centralised power to form a government for - only hundreds of policy governments (thousands regionally). A citizen has the true freedom to represent himself - whatever his beliefs are. They choose which policies pass and which don't. They get to create policies too. As mentioned earlier in the book, every person undergoes a certain level of cognitive dissonance in their belief system. They contain contradictory beliefs from different spheres of politics based on their life experiences.

However, with the advent of political parties, ideology has converted people with diverse thoughts into race-horses, only going in one direction. For example, Republicans in the US often believe in antivax, anti-mask, and other fringe theories, although their main reason for believing the Republicans maybe something else (conservative economics and nationalist perceptions). Free from this burden of choosing the better of two evils, citizens can genuinely impact their lives and create a better world.

Politics, But Simpler

People don't care about everything. Often, it's not because we don't want to; we can't. So, blaming people for being ambivalent about your struggle is pointless when they have no power to change how the world thinks. We can help them understand, but words don't move walls. But in a democracy, when a person votes, they don't vote about the topics which matter to them. Instead, they vote for everything - at once! The Webocracy changes that. Now, people will only vote how they care.

In addition, since every person in your target region must understand your policy, you have to phrase it, so everyone gets it. So, it has to be simple - without all the legal jargon. If you make an immensely wordy treatise which displays your lacking connection to the ordinary person, your policy will not pass. Everyone can genuinely understand the laws they voted for the first time without needing a lawyer.

There's No One Left to Bribe

Today, a significant problem afflicting governments everywhere is corruption. Everyone has seen some instance of this, I am sure. Perhaps you witnessed your local cop take a bribe from a helmet-less motorcyclist.

You might have read about members of your country's cabinet accepting bribes from a defence contractor. The apparent problem with corruption is that it's illegal, unfair and inefficient. Nobody wants to be at the behest of a corrupt cop, let alone a corrupt government. Yet we all are anyway.

However, in a nation of constant checks and the lack of any actual government, there is no one left to bribe. You can't bribe an algorithm, and indeed not a policy government we can easily overthrow if they take the bribe. So, the Webocracy is the most efficient form of government.

Conclusion

The Webocracy is a radical idea; we'll need time to develop its infrastructure (a few years). Then, with the support of the world, perhaps we will truly create a system of Webocracy, saving our planet from the catastrophe we are nearing. You may say that things are not as bad as they sound - we aren't on the brink of apocalypse. I agree. But I am sure we are tired of the inaction of our gilded age. Society has made us into flies caught in the web of a vicious spider: social inertia. We cannot get out of its binds without struggling - but we also don't want to escape these binds only to fall to our deaths. The Webocracy is our way out. Then, finally, people will get the chance to be Idealists and truly change our society. Let's stand up and save the world.

PART XII

The dragons and giants rejoiced: the beast was dead. They could finally be at peace. The tiny dragon shrugged off the boiling tears from his eyes. They had done it! But the mighty dragon was suspicious. What if, they thought, the future held more issues? What if it held more beasts? They decided that there was no reason to stop his self-improvement. The mighty dragon began to improve himself, readying himself for the future. They would become the beast, the guard of this society.

Superhumanity

Or, What's the Future

> *'The advance of genetic engineering makes it quite conceivable that we will begin to design our own evolutionary process.'*
>
> – Isaac Asimov

Who hasn't wanted to have superpowers once? From the time we were primitive cavemen to today in the digital era, we have always fantasised about a creature more powerful than us - djinns, gods, superheroes, et cetera. We have created whole mythologies, folklores and literary universes based on our understanding of superior creatures. But, for most of our existence, they have remained just that: stories. However, soon, we will possess the capability to create superhumans potentially. From more intelligent life to larger lifespans (possibly amortal) people, healthier humans to physically advanced ones. All that from birth. That raises one serious question: should we genetically engineer these superhumans?

Are You Superhuman?

Firstly, we must understand what a superhuman means. A superhuman is a person who has advanced abilities of some kind from birth. By this definition, we include various prodigies from across all fields - Leonardo da Vinci, Chanakya, Usain Bolt, Albert Einstein, et cetera. However, we can argue that they possessed a slight genetic variation which brought about such a prodigious personality. Hence, we can define superhumans as people born with vastly significant differences in physical/mental/emotional abilities than usual humans. Assuming we can engineer such genetic changes (which we do in some part as I write this), we must understand the primary motivations of such a personality. All in all, the possibilities of their behaviour can be divided into three as acutely depicted in literature before.

1. A human with powers - For example, Stan Lee's Spider-Man.
2. A God-born Human - For instance, William Marston's Wonder Woman
3. A God - For example, Alan Moore's Dr Manhattan

The Marvel Fans

The first category, 'Humans with powers', is one we can witness today. From the sense-enabled Isao Machii to memory genius Stephen Wiltshire, forever running Dean Karnazes to the electricity controlling Slavisa Pajkic, there have potentially been many thousands of humans with such abilities throughout history. They possess the same motivations as humans and are technically no different. Just like Spider-Man, their powers do not change their intentions - although they intend to use them. Peter Parker and Bruce Wayne coped similarly to their guardians' deaths: by becoming superheroes. This category of people will not disrupt society if slowly introduced into the general population (if genetically engineered). They possess generally subtle abilities which are less intimidating at first glance. These include slightly advanced intelligence, better physique, more resistance to infections and others like them. These abilities exist today and could be our society's future if we slowly go down the path of genetic engineering humans.

The DC Fans

The second category is 'God-born human'. In our current world, such people do not exist (to my knowledge). They have extraordinary and visible abilities making them grossly different from a human. Such people have a mixture of mastery - advanced intelligence, high levels of disease resistance, longer lifespan, better physique, defined appearance and other miscellaneous powers. Like Wonder Woman, they do not fit in with society even if they try. They are noticeable and thus intimidating. Any number of such superhumans would disrupt the functioning of society if known. However, a carefully planted system of such people could enable a highly evolved society to come about within centuries. However, change will be drastic and dissonant. It could also result in further alienation of the superhumans, which would be disastrous to nearby society due to the powers possessed by the superhumans.

The Watchmen Fans

The third category is 'God'. We cannot create this category yet. Perhaps a century later, we will be able to. Just as once people believed God created man, we may do the reverse. Man creates God. Just like Dr Manhattan, these superhumans will be destructive to current human society. They do not care particularly about humans. These superhumans have advanced abilities beyond what we think can be genetically engineered today.

Should We Create Superior Life

So, should we genetically engineer humans? Let us first look at the advantages:

1. Lower death rates.
2. More significant advancements in technology, society, and the limits of humanity.
3. More cohesive community of more perfect humans.
4. Longer lives, disease resistance, higher intelligence and other such abilities.
5. Lesser food/water required.

What are the disadvantages of these superhumans, and how do we solve them?

1. **Longer lives** - Population problems may arise. There may be problems with maintaining jobs or requiring more food and resources.

2. **Different societal classes** - Only the rich would initially be able to afford such a technique, leading to the physical cementing of such a disparity between classes forever.

3. **Reduce genetic diversity** - Genes do not work in a binary fashion; they only influence solitary characteristics. In various combinations, genes can have both positive and negative effects. By eliminating specific genes, one prevents such helpful diversity from arising. A reduced gene pool would also result in the prevention of natural evolution.

4. **Trait selection** - People would be able to choose what traits their child has. Read the chapter on free will.

5. **Creation of genetic weapons** - People could be grown to be loyal super soldiers for a country.

Superhuman Sinners

How do we rectify such a crisis? We ban such experimentation. We prevent the growth of superhumanity primarily because the costs direly outweigh the benefits in current society. However, we cannot stop the flow of science and technology for long. Eventually, progress will have to happen, and we will choose. It is essential to make these choices on our terms and not on those of the situations we face. If we are not careful, there may come a time when climate change, food insecurity, lack of natural resources and wars will lead us into a fourth global arms race. From our collective experiences with gunpowder, nuclear weapons and cyberwar, we must be aware of the gravity of such a situation. The fourth arms race may well be about superhumans. We cannot possess and utilise the power of superhumanity if we do not stand united within a single entity. Unlike gunpowder, computers and missiles, superhumans are people: they may be the most powerful weapon or the most powerful tool. A superhuman is a natural person with motivations far more complex than obeying the laws of physics. Morally speaking, it is vital to prevent the weaponisation of humans, making them mere equivalents of living missiles.

When we possess a Webocracy with a united world (in some fashion), we could introduce superhumans into society slowly, letting them live with neutral, average families worldwide. They would only possess slightly advanced abilities to increment over time. While exceptionally fast compared to natural selection and evolution, this process would take many generations, moving the distribution curve of the property's appearance towards the right. Problems 1, 2, 4 and 5 are solved if the Webocracy takes charge of this and spreads superhumans worldwide in diverse backgrounds.

As the meaning of work changes, jobs will continue to exist. These superhumans will also use fewer resources than the average human. The Webocracy chooses a set of socially beneficial traits, so trait selection and societal division will not be a negative externality. In addition, as these abilities accumulate over generations, changes will not be instantaneously noticeable. Still, we will have a brighter, fitter, healthier population in the long run - a sort of engineered evolution. Point 3 is a critical downside to the genetic engineering of humans. However, the generation-spanning nature of this work implies that there will be sufficient time for studies to note changes and adjust the gene-editing tool in use in the future.

The future is either exceptionally bright or dismally ignominious for superhumans. Inevitably, the world will have superhumans. Which kind and what their motivations will be, one can only speculate. Perhaps this speculation will come into use in the future. The need to adapt to change is constant and unchanging in an ever-changing landscape like this planet. As our world enters another phase of life, our dwindling resources, climate change, and various problems are catching up with us. We must take specific measures to ensure that the human (or superhuman) race continues beyond extinction.

Predicting the Future

Or, How Did I Write This Book

> *'I was not predicting the future, I was trying to prevent it.'*
> — *Ray Bradbury*

Disclaimer: This chapter doesn't add to the substance of the concept of Idealism. However, it's the methodology based on which I've predicted the future and come up with many solutions mentioned in the previous chapters. Therefore, you can skip this chapter if you want: it won't alter the book's meaning.

Predicting the future has always been a very sought-after talent - from peasants in the Dark Ages to stockbrokers today. Our innate urge to know how the future lies has always troubled our species. Misused by various charlatans, religious godmen and soothsayers, the art of forecasting is often seen as merely educated guesswork and shots in the dark. Today, there is a relatively more scientific approach to intuiting what lies ahead - futurology.

However, any change in the direction towards studying the times to come has not changed, with most predictions still being open-ended and inconclusive. Naturally, some predictions come true, but mere guessing does not predict the world order. A more comprehensive future analysis must be made and not solely based on past trends. While statistics and current trends are vital to factor in, the future is uncertain because various unseen, unknown or unthought connections between fields and utter randomness pervades it.

For this reason, I have decided to depart from this strange tradition of guessing. Instead, as I have written this book, I performed a meticulous analysis based on various causal links between current and future developments (to the best of my abilities). For this, I will use five major principles - 4 newly hypothesised and one age-old concept.

1. The Butterfly Effect, Chaos Theory
2. Temporal Entropy
3. The Future Uncertainty Principle
4. The Science Fiction Bias
5. The Prediction Path Diagram (PPD)

The Butterfly Effect

In chaos theory, the butterfly effect is the idea that small events can have non-linear impacts on a chaotic, complex system. Here, we refer to the timeline of the world - the past, present and the future - as being our very complex system. Stories of the butterfly effect in real life surround us everywhere. Small events have influenced our lives, from chance romances to serendipitous meetings. After it, the interaction of our circumstantial free will causes the butterfly effect, as explained in the chapter on free will. As we speak, a person who will profoundly impact your life by proxy may have been born. Perhaps it is a future prime minister or revolutionary, Nobel laureate or messiah (in case this is someone famous soon, the date I wrote this was 5th March 2022). A person's birth is a relatively minor event, although significantly more critical than tossing a ball or taking a picture.

Our world does not change because of important things like wars and crises but small things which cause them. A bomb does not drop itself: it's a conscious action with many routes in history due to the coincidence of some factors. However, predicting these factors is virtually impossible. For example, kicking a solitary stone can puncture a tire, killing a driver, thus toppling a massive financial dynasty. Yet, you cannot have predicted such an outcome. That is the result of the effect: a small event can have virtually no effect either. Thus, an event can either change the course of history or do nothing at all. And there's no way to tell the difference before it happens. Therefore, we often overlook this factor in analysing the future.

Temporal Entropy

In future analysis, we should not be concerned with predicting the exact small event that will affect our future. Instead, we should grapple with the (approximate) probability of the scenarios. In other words, we should be concerned about the temporal entropy in the system.

Entropy is a scientific term referring to the degree of disorder in a system. It is a concept used in various sciences, from thermodynamics to telecommunication. However, until now, entropy has not been used to predict the future. Temporal entropy refers to the degree of randomness or unpredictability in the future. Any given point in time can be in the past, the present or the future. The present is merely the flux of moments in time changing from their future state to their past state. Thus, in reality, a point can be said to be either in the future state or the past state. To add on, it can either be in one form or change between the two.

Once it becomes the past, a point in time has already happened and cannot be changed. As it has become entirely static, we can 'predict' it with 100% accuracy. Thus, the entropy of a point in time in the past is null. On the contrary, any point in time set in the future state can have a higher degree of entropy above null. Now, unlike in other fields, predicting the future is not an exact science, and we can only work in the fashion of relatives. However, to accurately compare relative entropy over time, we must imagine that we are in the past, looking at the future. The general direction for entropy in human civilisation has gradually decreased over time, with a sharp reduction in the last 300 years.

What are the rules of temporal entropy?

1. The likelihood of random events occurring is positive entropy.
2. Entropy decreases with an increase in order within the timeline.
3. Entropy increases with the number of free units in a timeline (i.e., units with free will).

In any analysis trying to predict the future, we must account for temporal entropy causing havoc. Events such as the COVID-19 pandemic, which appear to have erupted from seemingly nowhere, are proof of the importance of accounting for temporal entropy. Generally speaking, a society can willingly reduce its temporal entropy by inducing more order via regulation, political control, et cetera or vice versa. Naturally, such a law does not protect society from substantial changes: it just reduces the number of such possibilities. How many murders do we prevent because we have a working police force, for instance? The most definite way of reducing temporal entropy is by advancements in technology. With Vaccine X, we may never face massive problems in terms of pandemics. The Webocracy will change the idea of peace. With UBA, we may never face considerable difficulties in terms of poverty.

Generally, advanced societies with more protection against various threats tend to lower their temporal entropy. But, yet again, I must emphasise that a low temporal entropy does not imply a lower scale butterfly effect. Instead, it means fewer potential butterfly effects (to affect the nation, in this case).

Future Uncertainty Principle

As we learn from the concept of temporal entropy, the future is uncertain. However, to safeguard against inaccuracy, we can use a general empirical expression.

$$\Delta C \propto 1/\Delta T$$

Here, ΔC stands for the accuracy of the prediction, and ΔT stands for the accuracy of the period predicted. Here, accuracy refers to the vagueness/

definition of one's prediction. For example, if someone predicted a precise prediction, the chances are that the time expected is quite off. Similarly, if someone details an exact timing, the accuracy of the prediction may be quite off. That is a relatively intuitive notion. However, that is primarily an empirical trade-off.

This equation is analogous to the quantum mechanical Heisenberg Uncertainty Principle, in which the accuracy of the location of a particle is inversely proportional to the accuracy of its momentum.

This concept is quite crucial in defining how to make predictions. While we could all pretend to be Nostradamus and write vague verses predicting the future, we want specific predictions. However, one should not err on the side of either time or forecast in these situations.

Science Fiction Bias

Science-fiction, or more exclusively dystopian fiction, is a genre often showing us the grim realities which await us if we continue down our paths. Most books take a specific field and lead us to its graveyard to see how life becomes without it. For example, freedom in 1984 and Brave New World, reading in Fahrenheit 451 or patriarchy in the Handmaid's Tale. However, as many readers do fathom, such a world will most probably never exist - although similar policies may. The books are not explicit predictions. Instead, they are warnings. However, many analysts trying to predict the future often use the same approach as dystopian authors. They usually take a particular issue and push it to 20-50 years in the future, selectively considering the impact of other factors on it. They then think of different topics and try to adjust their draft prediction for these problems as well.

Many famous books (or authors) fall into the purview of this wrong approach. A common theme in such authors is their ability to ask questions so broad any answer (even a stupid one) is proper in a way. As a result, they are useless, vast assumptions like those Nostradamus makes. Unfortunately, these authors face no repercussions for their dangerous guesswork, which also influences policy development. Take Yuval Noah Harari, whose broad strokes at the future have resulted in impractical notion - major epidemics were all but over in the first world (COVID-19 happened soon after).

Such an approach is naturally problematic - it provides a person with a somewhat inaccurate prediction. Although some predictions may come true - being entirely vague or already in the works - even a broken watch tells the correct time twice a day. Unlike the average futuristic world of literature, the reality is complicated beyond any one person's understanding. Thus, falling into the science-fiction bias is a very human trait. We cannot fathom the multiple connections and possibilities which link the various fields of the future.

Prediction Path Diagrams

Unless that is, we could. Let's take a leaf out of causal inference. Prediction path diagrams are relative causal relationships between variables impacting the future. We can generally group the future variables into six major categories and temporal entropy.

1. Technology - Variables such as AI, Genetic Engineering, Organ farming, et cetera
2. Society - Variables such as Population growth, Literacy rate, Labour development, et cetera
3. Human - Variables such as Physical aptitude, life expectancy, living requirements, et cetera
4. Power Dynamics - Variables such as majority political opinions, geopolitical conflicts, government intervention, et cetera
5. Resources - Variables such as real estate, water, food, et cetera
6. Environment - Variables such as climate, biodiversity, habitats, et cetera

In causal inference theory, there is a fascinating trend of displaying relations between variables as path diagrams in the direction of causation.

Prediction path diagrams are a basic map for the various factors which may exist and their effects on other elements in the future.

Some of you may scoff at the idea, believing anyone can decipher these connections without needing this map. However, the more factors you account for, the more relationships arise, making the map for the future more confusing than ever. In addition, these diagrams may reveal paths which you would never have thought of before. This part of the book discusses the two significant PPDs - one based on today's timeline and one based on the idealist timeline.

Using These Principles

With these five principles, which feed into each other, you can successfully predict the future based on what data you have or would like to imagine. Firstly, understanding the butterfly effect is essential to how the future works. It is the main reason why the future uncertainty principle holds. The more specific you are, the less correct you will be. A general prediction should neither be too open-ended nor too specific. While predicting, we have to strike a balance and try to be accurate about the general direction of the future rather than the exactitudes of it. We must calculate temporal entropy (relative) concerning a standard average human year. An average human year consists of a moderate amount of disruption, a comparable level of development (thus, you cannot compare 2022 with 3022, but you can with 2122) and relative stability. For these chapters, this year is 2019 (2020 and 2021 do not count for quite obvious reasons). In addition, one must keep in mind prediction path diagrams and work their way across the web spun by the connections between various fields with data we have today.

Predicting the future is no mean feat. However, when done meticulously, it provides a fascinating insight into preparing for the future and how to change it. Thus, the following chapter will predict the future. Perhaps this will be a final nail in the coffin for arguments against Idealism. The future awaits.

Conclusion

Or, What Does Our Future Hold

'And this is the beginning of the end.'

– Guy Kawasaki

So, what does our future hold for us? Is it bright or abysmal, and how can we change our state of affairs? Let's first look at the factors involved. Predicting the future of the world is complex but plausible. Here are some of the significant predictions regarding the world. But, first, let's figure out the main fields that impact our society.

The Six Fields

1. **The Environment**

    a. The Climate
    b. The Biosphere
    c. Pollution Levels

2. **The Society**

    a. Population
    b. Morality and the Law
    c. Education
    d. Work

3. **The Resources**

    a. Labour
    b. Sustenance

    c. Energy

    d. Industrial

    e. Land

4. **The Technology**

    a. Organic

    b. Inorganic

5. **The Power Dynamics**

    a. Domestic Politics

    b. International Politics

    c. Conflict

    d. Economic System

    e. Morality and Law

6. **The Human**

    a. Labour

    b. Needs

    c. Aptitude

How Uncertain Are We?

In a word, very. It is now 2022, and our base typical year for calculating is 2019. Things seem to have gotten steadily unpredictable. In a single week, Shinzo Abe was assassinated, the Sri Lankan government fled, and Boris Johnson stepped down as the British PM and Tory leader. However, as mentioned before, all these incidents began with small unnoticeable changes, some of which evolved together. These events were impacted by many others - from the war between Russia and Ukraine to Tetsuya Yamagami's mother. So, what is our current level of temporal entropy compared to 2019? Higher. Why?

1. **COVID-19:** The current pandemic increases the chances of the butterfly effect. After all, tiny invisible killers are roaming

the air as we speak. The pandemic contributed to half of the increased entropy in 2022.

2. **Political instability:** So many nations face riots, coups and revolutions. This chaos leads to less order - a recipe for entropy. This instability contributed to an eighth of the increase.

3. **Economic crises:** Quite a few nations are going through financial and economic troubles. This instability makes people lose faith in their authorities; thus, there is no order. These crises contributed to a sixth of the rising entropy.

4. **International politics:** The world has faced several wars, and negotiations have failed. These problems cost us a fifth of the increase.

Although there were other causes, these majorly led to a higher temporal entropy in 2022 than in 2019, against the expected decrease. Perhaps it is because we move through phases of disorder (two steps forward, one step back).

Disclaimer to These Predictions

We get offended - even by facts. The other day, fans of an actor rioted because the man died (peacefully). The worst part is that what I say now is not fact: not yet, at least. So, I ask you to proceed with some caution. You may not believe me, and that is alright. However, to the best of my information and these principles, that is our future. I won't claim that we are facing societal ruin or destruction - we are not. Neither will I contend that we are approaching some beautiful end to history with some technological union. That's stupid. Let us not fall to the wiles of extremity and reasonably tell what is to come. What I'm writing is not about science fiction but reality. Please take it in such a fashion. Let us begin.

The Climate That Could Be

Let's get into what the roots of Climate Change are. Based on the PPD, I have gathered together this simple mechanism to define our sources:

I have actively supported the climate change movement for a long time. Yet, it appears that the way the future pans out, we will not face an apocalyptic climate event. However, this prediction is not an invitation to do nothing. Still, you meet your destiny on the path you take to avoid it. Without enacting Idealism, the future looks pretty dim - but not abysmal.

1. **Corporate Economics** - Corporate production is one of the most critical issues shaping the future of climate change. Since 1988, just 25 entities have produced more than half the world's industrial emissions. The worst are ExxonMobil, Shell, BP, Aramco and Chevron. Unfortunately, many nations (which contribute to the maximum emissions) have not placed viable checks on this production. The popular Carbon Tax/Emission Trading model adopted by much of the EU (and recently China) has not inspired global action. In the future, more countries will follow this model of revenue production. However, they will be severely discouraged by important lobbying partners: the fight between the power of votes and money has never been more distinct.

2. **Consumer Trends** - Moreover, as global populations grow aware of the immediate nature of climate change, consumer trends will shift dramatically. It's already begun! We must anticipate a remarkable shift coming at once (and not slowly), forcing fossil fuel producers to paint themselves a shade of green. Although the reaction will correlate to the per capita income of nations, the US will remain a notable exception, entering the fray only much later. Unfortunately, these changes will not become the norm until the next decade.

3. **Sustainable Lending** - Despite international pressure, the overall impact on fossil fuel levels will be limited. The maximum effect will arrive as conditional aid. As economies fall to debt, international lenders will begin demanding climate regulations - especially in Europe, Asia and Latin America. The US will

consistently remain resilient to these forces, only swaying to domestic morality (which will be responsible for the bravado of these corporations).

4. **Declining Emissions** - Industrial resources responsible for increased emissions will continue to decline in usage after peaking within the decade. As a result, climate change will continue, but global warming will slow down. No, this slowing down is not natural - it is due to human causes. Human actions have caused this change (thanks to consumers and politics).

5. **Climate Change Technology** - However, all these efforts would be futile without already available climate technology and future developments. Many technologies can deal with climate change, most famously carbon capture. More radically, we could try to reverse climate change by refreezing the poles or fertilising the oceans. The future of the world lies in the hands of technology. Yet, as we have seen, the world loves to ignore science (especially the people in charge): we've seen it with endangered animals, and we've seen it with religion.

6. **Rising Sea Levels** - As time progresses, the rising sea levels will begin engulfing more landmasses. Thankfully, the world will be ready. Or at least the rich (and semi-rich) countries will be. At this moment, nations will realise the need to come together: yet they will only move further apart. This state of affairs will have effects discussed below.

In summation, the world will face severe economic, cultural and moral crises as climate change goes unattended. The repercussions of global discord will be catastrophic, delaying action due to their sense of self-security. Technology will save us, but without international consensus, its efforts will be (in the end) minute. Although the crisis will prolong beyond our planet's current expiration date, climate change will inevitably cause problems of a large magnitude.

The Biosphere That Could Be

Our failure to effectively deal with the climate issue will lead to problems for our biodiversity. But how exactly? Let's refer to our PPD.

1. **Declining Pollution Rates** - The pollutants in our environment are toxic not only to us but also to animals. However, from sound to land, water to air, the annual rate of pollution is decreasing. While it is not reducing the total, this is excellent news! Moreover, this trend will continue throughout the next few decades, thanks to consumer awareness, environmental regulation (both nationally and internationally) and new technology.

2. **International Organisation** - Although lacking real power, international organisations have proven to be critical to the effort to save flora and fauna from extinction. However, as national collaboration begins to fray (owing to the changing trends of populism and democracy), these efforts will continue without significant headway into the next decade.

3. **Technology** - Like everywhere else, technology will be critical to the biosphere's future. Even when the scientific community invests in complex methods of saving species, such as gene sequencing and drone conservation, politics will prevent large-scale usage. Many of the world's most biodiverse countries - especially India and Brazil - will face an uphill task. New technologies will develop throughout the future, but governments will severely delay implementing them in critical biodiversity zones worldwide.

4. **Corporate Irresponsibility** - Once again, the 'beautiful' system of Capitalism comes to haunt us. Here, the habitats of many animals are endangered by corporations such as Nestle, Hershey and Kellogg's. By taking over tracts of forest and converting them into single-crop plantations, companies are responsible for destroying vast ecosystems, endangering many species - both legally and illegally. As developing countries try to open

their nations to the global capitalist order, they face a race to the bottom. This race towards deregulation is harmful and will cause the mass destruction of biodiversity and the extinction of species (which may include the Javan rhinos and Sumatran tigers, amongst others). The Living Planet Index will continue to fall, and despite popular opinion, corporations will merely greenwash themselves.

5. **Conflict** - As military conflicts rise, especially with unaccountable actors, habitats will continue to be converted into battlegrounds, where human needs will, unfortunately, trump animal ones. Conservation often takes a backseat to politics.

In general, the biosphere is up for some of its roughest decades without intervention by Idealist forces - foremost of which is the Extinction Rebellion.

The Morals That Could Be

What about our ideas of virtue and vice? What about our opinions? Referring to the PPDs, we see the usual generational shift and an interesting political one.

1. **Generational Shift** - The latest generation of humanity, just becoming adults, has adopted an overwhelmingly liberal and welcoming view of politics. We can also expect this shift in morality to continue in the next generation. This trend is due to the profound levels of cultural diversity, education and the Internet. So naturally, we can also see the Flynn Effect, the increase in average IQ over a sustained basis, causing a change in our understandings.

2. **The Internet** - As the Internet reaches the entire world, we will see the rise of self-censorship and Cancel culture, in addition to the explosion of globalisation. The future is unkind to political opinions it considers of another age. Within the following decades, homosexuality, equality and many other liberal

movements will become normalised. The Internet will shape the lives and opinions of today's children in myriad ways. Yes, this influence has its benefits, but it comes at the cost of free and original thought.

3. **The Demographic Shift** - The world is globalising - and with economic changes come cultural ones. People are immigrating much more than ever before (the number of immigrants is three times that of 1970). But Pakistani-American immigrants will not have the same political views as African-Americans. They carry Pakistani culture and similarly influenced beliefs. Thus, with immigration rising in the following decades, we can anticipate a more leftward shift on topics such as immigration and foreign policy, but rightward changes on homosexuality, xenophobia, et cetera. However, since the world works as a democracy, we will perceive this shift as solely leftward.

In conclusion, our morality will tend to the left, as all of history has done. However, unlike in the past, we will have help from the Internet to let our opinions reach the world.

The Population That Could Be

With today's fertility rates starting to drop (mostly in developed countries), it seems as though the population explosion will come into our control soon. Naturally, this is because of our efforts in the future (note that this isn't a purely statistical prediction). The main trends which drive this population change are as follows.

1. **Education** - Yes, education is vital in many ways towards decreasing fertility rates. We learn (quite literally) the basics of family planning and using contraception. Less directly, educating women leads to more effective child-rearing since this task often ends up in the hands of women in many countries. Additionally, education leads to better aptitude and technology, which in turn helps create the facilities required to decrease populations. The

future is exceptionally bright for education (if not for all else) in terms of literacy. Thus, we can expect a population decline.

2. **Capitalism** - Sadly, as countries become more capitalist, the poor are left more exposed and neglected. Because of the terrible mix of high mortality and fertility, the poor cannot move beyond their vicious cycle of wage labour and procreation. Hence, in the future (as we already know), less developed nations will have a higher fertility rate. This problem will increase in the next decade, causing mortality to rise due to the rapid deregulation of developing economies.

3. **Globalisation** - The trend of globalisation has led to a world of open economies and relatively open borders (yes). The world is more open to immigrants than it has ever been. Yes, there are problems like border control and refugee crises. However, no matter how many Trump-like politicians we find, the world is undoubtedly more accessible than a century ago. This trend of globalisation will continue rapidly in the following decades (with some economic incentive), leading to a vast intermixing of cultures and ethnicities. This diversity will change the composition of many nations, much to the horror of supremacists.

So, we can expect a stable population with very diverse people on this planet in the future. This trend implies a gross change in political opinions, as we explained earlier.

The Education That Could Be

The future of education is bright (in terms of statistics). However, it is woefully underprepared to cope with globalisation, amongst other immediate crises.

1. **Globalisation/Nationalisation** - Textbooks today from state syllabi are often somewhat politically influenced - at least in not-so-full democracies. Sometimes it is blatant, while at

others times, people can live their lives without knowing the subtle hints the government dropped. However, this disparity will haunt us in the future, in a society where our political opinions find extremity on the Internet. Thus, our future is bleak and filled with self-censorship and nationalist primacy. This disturbing trend of politicised education has previously narrowed society and will do so in the future, upsetting our leftward shift in politics.

2. **The Flynn Effect and Rising Aptitude** - Humans are growing more intelligent (IQ), as we previously noted.

3. **Increased Political Focus** - Education has become an international focal point. While college education will continue to gather around the West in terms of absolute prestige, colleges will continue to rise everywhere. From Botswana to India, the rise of colleges will lead to an unparalleled level of education in this world, helping usher us into the next era of science and politics.

The Technology That Could Be

Today, we live in a world where technology seems to have a solution to everything. Why? There are many reasons, as I have listed below. But will this trend continue in the future? Hopefully, yes. The more important question is whether this technology will be helpful.

1. **Ethics** - I am not one to hinder ethics even when science is at stake. However, science is severely hampered by our rising awareness of morality. Although we have noble intentions for preventing human genetic engineering and embryonic stem cell research, they may often spring from a binary view of the issue. With the Internet, scientific research into new fields faces severe threats. Uninformed, scared people will condemn ideas that severely affect organic and inorganic technologies. Sadly, this trend will only increase dramatically in the future. Human morality, sometimes misplaced, will prevent scientific discovery.

2. **Capitalism** - As we noted in the chapter on Unisism, Capitalism has the unique trend of inspiring and stifling innovation. In the future, I anticipate perfunctory creation on the part of MNCs, with genuine ground-breaking innovations, bought out. So, we can expect the regular cycle of economics to thrive on the side of personal gain and social loss.

3. **Education** - The world is receiving more education than ever. The world, from Asia to America, is inching towards tertiary education. Although the focus will remain on STEM subjects, teaching in the future will be more diverse (but digital-oriented). This trend benefits technology, producing some of our world's finest engineers, doctors, et cetera. Thus, education will result in accessible technology, subject to political restraint.

The Peace That Could Be

No. Our world will not see peace. Nations will show cracks, and people will revolt. However, on the bright side, these conflicts will grow less deadly.

1. **Land** - Since time immemorial, land (and more importantly, the resources it contains) has been invaluable to people. However, our land will become critical with rising sea levels, changing ecosystems and shifting demographics. Thus, land and resources will shape the gross increase in conflicts in the following decades.

2. **International Order** - International Organisations like the UN will continue to grow more irrelevant, falling in line with the money of developed nations. Bribery is legal in international terms ('conditional aid'), so no real action is taken against those who have the resources to defy (like China, the USA, Russia, et cetera). This lack of concern for regulation will only encourage more nations to rush toward conflict. From the Middle East to Europe, India to the South China Sea, battles are just waiting to happen (however, only one/two of these regions will explode

into war since the world tends to focus on either single wars or hundreds at once).

3. **Education** - Thankfully, education can lead to a safer world - often allowing us to see our options and predict. With education, we can create a better future in terms of health, life, law, et cetera. However, wrong education can also make military technology, propaganda-filled minds, or worse. The world can take either path. However, it appears as though flawed democracies will choose the former with autocracies.

4. **Economics** - Although economic systems like Capitalism, in theory, should offer incentives against war, this doesn't work out in reality. Capitalist free trade has its positives for a nation. However, is that enough to prevent a war? No. Conflicts exist for many reasons - land, resources, politics, et cetera. Sadly, Capitalism causes their problems. Thus, by focusing on such an economy, we cannot see its indirect effects on the causes of war. Nevertheless, this economic system will be the root of many conflicts in the future.

The world is getting more aggressive. Without Idealism, we may soon live in a world of constant, loud conflict. Yes, even worse than the one we are in today.

The Economy That Could Be

As the business cycle shortens, things are getting out of hand. Every year, we see another country joining the ranks of the economically affected. Why?

1. **Resource Scarcity** - Naturally, the basis of economics is the question of scarcity. Even here, the same question plagues us as land, resources, and populations change. However, this resource loss is uniform globally - and the wealthier nations have the money to buy their way out. The less developed economies do

not. This disparity will be the source of the world's economic troubles in the future.

2. **Conflict** - Similarly, war will result in a broken-down economic system. As the world progresses through the decade, we can expect reluctant global trade between parties causing general hardships for the commoner.

As we already discussed in the chapter on Unisism, the global economy will face terrible hardships in the future, primarily due to its laissez-faire, Capitalist approach.

Conclusion

I will not be apocalyptic. The world is not going to the dogs - it's worse. However, we won't be extinct in the century. So, there is an urgent need for change, but not reactionary change. It's time for a consolidated plan of action: a plan I just detailed in this book.

Idealism is about change. The future is ours to make, although, in a way, it's already decided. Throughout the book, I have proposed many radical concepts. Can it be done? Can we have a Webocracy or Unisist system? Yes! The world needs idealists: hopefully, you're one of them. So, I have only one question left to ask you: will you save the world? For you, it's now or never.

The world is watching you, reader. If you choose to change what you wish to change, I have no doubt that the future will be benefitted. There is only one judge, after all, of human character - history. We must be resilient and courageous in the face of the many adversities that lie ahead. We must confront the problems of the world and try our best to help the most we can. After all, Idealism is the idea of ideals. Where would we be without our ideals?

Epilogue

Congratulations, you've reached the end of this book. So, what now? What will you do, free of the burden of reading this book? Perhaps you have some lingering questions. Or maybe you don't like what I've written. Probably both. My dad once told me (regarding this book) that a person may agree with a majority of my ideas - but he would be hard pressed to find someone who agreed with all. Subject to change in the future - I hope!

Importantly, you have to think. What have you learnt, and what will you do? Will you learn from the book, or is this just another book lying in your cupboard? This time, I hope it will be different. Will you grow wings? Can you?

The dragon within you is waiting. So shut up and spread your wings. Or let the problems roll over you - killing your dragon. The dragon needs wings. Let's get to work.

References

'The references you do not verify are the good ones.'

– Charles Peguy

1. Andrews, Peter. "Last Common Ancestor of Apes and Humans: Morphology and Environment." Folia Primatologica, vol. 91, no. 2, Feb. 2019, pp. 122–48, https://doi.org/10.1159/000501557.

2. Smith, Tanya M., et al. "Earliest Evidence of Modern Human Life History in North African Early Homo Sapiens." Proceedings of the National Academy of Sciences, vol. 104, no. 15, Apr. 2007, pp. 6128–33, https://doi.org/10.1073/pnas.0700747104.

3. Mendez, Fernando L., et al. "An African American Paternal Lineage Adds an Extremely Ancient Root to the Human Y Chromosome Phylogenetic Tree." The American Journal of Human Genetics, vol. 92, no. 3, Mar. 2013, pp. 454–59, https://doi.org/10.1016/j.ajhg.2013.02.002,

4. Endicott, Phillip, et al. "Evaluating the Mitochondrial Timescale of Human Evolution." Trends in Ecology & Evolution, vol. 24, no. 9, Sept. 2009, pp. 515–21, https://doi.org/10.1016/j.tree.2009.04.006.

5. "Occupy Wall Street | Anthropology of Contemporary Issues." Colby.edu, 2022, https://web.colby.edu/contemporary-issues/occupy-wall-street.

6. "25. Mali/Tauregs (1960-Present)." Uca.edu, 2019, https://uca.edu/politicalscience/dadm-project/sub-saharan-africa-region/malitauregs-1960-present.

7. Jean-Philippe Béja, et al. "Liu Xiaobo, Charter 08 and the Challenges of Political Reform in China." ResearchGate, unknown, July 2012, www.researchgate.net/publication/297488426_Liu_Xiaobo_Charter_08_and_the_Challenges_of_Political_Reform_in_China.

8. "Guillermo Fariñas Hernández - Human Rights Foundation." Human Rights Foundation, 2020, https://hrf.org/speakers/guillermo-farinas-hernandez/.

9. WALLACE, BRIAN. "NANA SAHIB in BRITISH CULTURE and MEMORY." The Historical Journal, vol. 58, no. 2, May 2015, pp. 589–613, https://doi.org/10.1017/s0018246x14000430.

10. De, Cuadernos. La Rebelión de Los Indígenas Bajo La Dirección de Pablo Presbere (Talamanca 1709-1710). no. 21, 2011, pp. 1409–3138, https://repositorio.ucr.ac.cr/bitstream/handle/10669/13284/1969-3088-1-SM.pdf?sequence=1&isAllowed=y.

11. Fairweather, Nicolas. "Hitler and Hitlerism: Germany under the Nazis." The Atlantic, theatlantic, 20 Apr. 1932, www.theatlantic.com/magazine/archive/1932/04/hitler-and-hitlerism-germany-under-the-nazis/308961/.

12. A Dictionary of British History. Oxford University Press, 2009, www.oxfordreference.com/view/10.1093/acref/9780199550371.001.0001/acref-9780199550371.

13. Moochi, Javid, et al. Market Reforms of Ala-Ud-Din Khilji. http://ijmess.org/assets/front_end/uplodes/gallery/JK1587_SS.pdf.

14. Collins, Francis S., and Jonathan Davis. The Language of God: A Scientist Presents Evidence for Belief. Howes - Clipper, 2008.

15. Dawkins, Richard. The God Delusion. London Black Swan, 2006.

16. "Sia Is the 21st Century's Most Resilient Songwriter." NPR.org, 6 Nov. 2018, www.npr.org/2018/11/06/664395501/sia-is-the-21st-centurys-most-resilient-songwriter.

17. Vevo. "Ed Sheeran - Shape of You (Live from the 59th Grammy Awards)." YouTube, 13 Feb. 2017, www.youtube.com/watch?v=uPvARJW_iVI.

18. Akhtar, Allana. "Some Americans Were Primed for Vaccine Skepticism after Decades of Mistrust in Big Pharma." Business Insider, Business Insider India, 24 Oct. 2021, www.businessinsider.in/science/health/news/some-americans-were-primed-for-vaccine-skepticism-after-decades-of-mistrust-in-big-pharma/articleshow/87241278.cms.

19. Bar, Shmuel. The Religious Sources of Islamic Terrorism the Religious Sources of Islamic Terrorism. June 2004, www.aclu.org/sites/default/files/field_document/ACLURM001331.pdf.

20. "General Dwight D. Eisenhower's Order of the Day (1944)." National Archives, 22 Sept. 2021, www.archives.gov/milestone-documents/general-eisenhowers-order-of-the-day.

21. Al Jazeera. "New Caledonia Rejects Independence from France in Third Vote." Aljazeera.com, Al Jazeera, 12 Dec. 2021, www.aljazeera.com/news/2021/12/12/new-caledonia-rejects-independence-from-france-in-third-vote.

22. "Kanak Socialist National Liberation Front | Political Party, New Caledonia | Britannica." Encyclopædia Britannica, 2022, www.britannica.com/topic/Kanak-Socialist-National-Liberation-Front.

23. "Exploring Occupy Wall Street's 'Adbuster' Origins." NPR.org, 20 Oct. 2011, www.npr.org/2011/10/20/141526467/exploring-occupy-wall-streets-adbuster-origins.

24. Sarah Van Gelder. This Changes Everything : Occupy Wall Street and the 99% Movement. Berrett-Koehler Publishers, 2011.

25. LEES, J. (2015). "A Character to Lose": Richard Goodlad, the Rangpur dhing, and the priorities of the East India Company's early colonial administrators. Journal of the Royal Asiatic Society, 25(2), 301–315. http://www.jstor.org/stable/43307694.

26. "Why Did the Indian Mutiny Happen? | National Army Museum." Nam.ac.uk, 2022, www.nam.ac.uk/explore/why-did-indian-mutiny-happen.

27. Guardian staff reporter. "Adolf Hitler and the Beer Hall Putsch." The Guardian, The Guardian, 9 Nov. 2015, www.theguardian.com/world/2015/nov/09/hitler-adolf-coup-bavaria-munich-government-german-1923.

28. Cusick, James. "Copernicus and Scientific Revolutions." ResearchGate, unknown, 24 Mar. 2007, www.researchgate.net/publication/327862242_Copernicus_and_Scientific_Revolutions.

29. Blair, Ann. "Tycho Brahe's Critique of Copernicus and the Copernican System." Journal of the History of Ideas, vol. 51, no. 3, July 1990, p. 355, https://doi.org/10.2307/2709620.

30. Babak Amini. (2016). A Brief History of the Dissemination and Reception of Karl Marx's Capital in the United States and Britain. World Review of Political Economy, 7(3), 334–349. https://doi.org/10.13169/worlrevipoliecon.7.3.0334.

31. "How Status Quo Bias Affects Your Decisions." *ThoughtCo*, 2018, www.thoughtco.com/status-quo-bias-4172981.

32. Satyanath, Shanker, et al. "Bowling for Fascism: Social Capital and the Rise of the Nazi Party in Weimar Germany, 1919-33." *SSRN Electronic Journal*, 2013, 10.2139/ssrn.2284907.

33. Angus Maddison, and Organisation For Economic Co-Operation And Development. *The World Economy : Historical Statistics*. Paris, Oecd, 2003.

34. Smith, Adam. *The Theory of Moral Sentiments*. Oxford, Clarendon, 24, 1759.

35. Smith, Adam. *The Wealth of Nations*. London, Penguin Books, 9 Mar. 1776.

36. Orwell, George. Nineteen Eighty-Four. Penguin Books, 1971.

37. F Scott Fitzgerald. Crack-Up. Alma Classics, 2018.

38. American Bible Society. The Holy Bible : Containing the Old and New Testaments ; Translated out of the Original Tongues

and with the Former Translations Diligently Compared and Revised. American Bible Society, 1986.

39. The Quran. Quran Institute, 2007, Surah Adh-Dhariyat [51:56].

40. Vedas, and J Muir. [Translations from the Vedas. By J. Muir.]. Pp. Iv. 96. [Privately Printed]: Edinburgh, 1873.

41. Richard Dawkins. The God Delusion. London Black Swan, 2006.

42. John Stuart Mill. Utilitarianism. Parker, Son and Bourn, 1861.

43. Richard Dawkins. The Selfish Gene. Oxford University Press, 1976.

44. Friedrich Wilhelm Nietzsche, and Thomas Common. Thus Spake Zarathustra. Modern Library Publ, 1905.

45. M Mitchell Waldrop. Complexity : The Emerging Science at the Edge of Order and Chaos. Simon & Schuster, 1993.

46. Mander, William. "Pantheism (Stanford Encyclopedia of Philosophy)." *Stanford.edu*, 2012, plato.stanford.edu/entries/pantheism.

47. "Deism | Definition, History, Beliefs, Significance, & Facts | Britannica." Encyclopædia Britannica, 2022, www.britannica.com/topic/Deism.

48. Cranney, Stephen. "Do People Who Believe in God Report More Meaning in Their Lives? The Existential Effects of Belief." *Journal for the Scientific Study of Religion*, vol. 52, no. 3, Sept. 2013, pp. 638–646, 10.1111/jssr.12046. Accessed 24 Apr. 2020.

49. Bhardwaj, Ananya. "'We Step in When Our Women Step out with Muslim Men' — How up Law Empowers Hindu Bully Groups." ThePrint, 26 Dec. 2020, theprint.in/india/we-operate-freely-now-how-hindu-groups-are-driving-ups-crackdown-on-love-jihad/574368/.

50. Express News Service. "Bajrang Dal Men Charge SC Members with Conversion..." The New Indian Express, The New Indian Express, 30 Dec. 2021, www.newindianexpress.com/states/karnataka/2021/dec/30/bajrang-dalmen-charge-sc-members-with-conversion-2401118.html.

51. "Aleph | History & Facts | Britannica." Encyclopædia Britannica, 2022, www.britannica.com/topic/Aleph.

52. "Islamic State in Iraq and the Levant | History, Leadership, & Facts | Britannica." Encyclopædia Britannica, 2022, www.britannica.com/topic/Islamic-State-in-Iraq-and-the-Levant.

53. "The Untold Story of the 'Circle of Trust' behind the World's First Gene-Edited Babies." Science.org, 2021, www.science.org/content/article/untold-story-circle-trust-behind-world-s-first-gene-edited-babies.

54. Aquinas, Thomas. [Summa Theologica]. Per Antonium Koburger - Impressa, 10 Oct. -29 Apr, 1477.

55. Hume, David, and Tom L. Beauchamp. An Enquiry Concerning Human Understanding : A Critical Edition. 1748. Clarendon Press, 2009.

56. Gottfried Wilhelm Leibniz. Discourse on Metaphysics. Manchester University Press, 1953.

57. Leucippus, et al. The Atomists, Leucippus and Democritus : Fragments : A Text and Translation with a Commentary. University Of Toronto Press, 2010.

58. Kaushanskaya, Margarita, et al. "The Effect of Second-Language Experience on Native-Language Processing." Vigo International Journal of Applied Linguistics, vol. 8, 2011, pp. 54–77, www.ncbi.nlm.nih.gov/pmc/articles/PMC3484981/.

59. McGue, Matt, and Irving I. Gottesman. "Behavior Genetics." The Encyclopedia of Clinical Psychology, Jan. 2015, pp. 1–11, https://doi.org/10.1002/9781118625392.wbecp578.

60. "How Can Identical Twins Turn out so Different?" NPR.org, 9 May 2013, www.npr.org/sections/health-shots/2013/05/14/182633402/how-can-identical-twins-turn-out-so-different.

61. Hong, L. E., et al. "A CHRNA5 allele Related to Nicotine Addiction and Schizophrenia." Genes, Brain and Behavior, vol. 10, no. 5, Apr. 2011, pp. 530–35, https://doi.org/10.1111/j.1601-183x.2011.00689.x.

62. Shin, Min-Jeong, et al. "Alcohol Consumption, Aldehyde Dehydrogenase 2 Gene Polymorphisms, and Cardiovascular Health in Korea." Yonsei Medical Journal, vol. 58, no. 4, 2017, p. 689, https://doi.org/10.3349/ymj.2017.58.4.689.

63. Rutger Bregman. HUMANKIND : A Hopeful History. Bloomsbury Publishing, 2021.

64. "Many Genes Influence Same-Sex Sexuality, Not a Single 'Gay Gene' (Published 2019)." *The New York Times*, 2022, www.nytimes.com/2019/08/29/science/gay-gene-sex.html.

65. Freedom From Religion, Inc. "The Pirahã: People Who Define Happiness without God: Daniel Everett - Freedom from Religion Foundation." Ffrf.org, 2022, ffrf.org/about/getting-acquainted/item/13492-the-pirahae-people-who-define-happiness-without-god.

66. Chatterjee, Amita. "Nyāya-Vaiśeṣika Philosophy." Oxford Handbooks Online, Oxford University Press, 2011, https://doi.org/10.1093/oxfordhb/9780195328998.003.0012.

67. www.semantico.com. "Jaina Philosophy : Routledge Encyclopedia of Philosophy Online." Archive.org, 2021, web.archive.org/web/20080705164341/www.rep.routledge.com/article/F005SECT3.

68. "Charvaka | Definition & Facts | Britannica." Encyclopædia Britannica, 2022, www.britannica.com/topic/Charvaka.

69. "Ajivika | Indian Sect | Britannica." Encyclopædia Britannica, 2022, www.britannica.com/topic/Ajivika.

70. "Mimamsa | Indian Philosophy | Britannica." Encyclopædia Britannica, 2022, www.britannica.com/topic/Mimamsa.

71. Konstan, David. "Epicurus (Stanford Encyclopedia of Philosophy)." Stanford.edu, 2018, https://plato.stanford.edu/entries/epicurus.

72. Taylor, C. C. W., and Mi-Kyoung Lee. "The Sophists (Stanford Encyclopedia of Philosophy)." Stanford.edu, 2020, https://plato.stanford.edu/entries/sophists.

73. Harari, Yuval Noah. Sapiens : A Brief History of Humankind. Harper Perennial, 2011.

74. Johnson, W. J. A Dictionary of Hinduism. United Kingdom, Oxford University Press.

75. Graham, Daniel W. "Heraclitus (Stanford Encyclopedia of Philosophy)." Stanford.edu, 2019, https://plato.stanford.edu/entries/heraclitus/.

76. "The Library : An Illustrated History" : Murray, Stuart, 1948.

77. Huylebrouck, Dirk. "Mathematics in (Central) Africa before Colonization." ResearchGate, unknown, 2006, www.researchgate.net/publication/265872061_Mathematics_in_central_Africa_before_colonization.

78. Pesch, and P.R. "The Dogon and Sirius." The Observatory, vol. 97, Feb. 1977, p. 26–28.

79. Dag Herbjørnsrud. "The Radical Philosophy of Egypt: Forget God and Family, Write!" Blog of the APA, 17 Dec. 2018, https://blog.apaonline.org/2018/12/17/the-radical-philosophy-of-egypt-forget-god-and-family-write/.

80. Hobson, John M. The Eastern Origins of Western Civilisation. Cambridge Univ. Press, 2011.

81. "How Islam Won, and Lost, the Lead in Science (Published 2001)." The New York Times, 2022, www.nytimes.com/2001/10/30/science/how-islam-won-and-lost-the-lead-in-science.html.

82. "Renaissance | Definition, Meaning, History, Artists, Art, & Facts | Britannica." Encyclopædia Britannica, 2022, www.britannica.com/event/Renaissance.

83. Fischer, Irmtraud, and Mercedes Navarro Puerto. Torah. Society Of Biblical Literature, 2014.

84. Parker, Kim, and Ruth Igielnik. "On the Cusp of Adulthood and Facing an Uncertain Future: What We Know about Gen Z so Far." Pew Research Center's Social & Demographic Trends Project, Pew Research Center's Social & Demographic Trends Project, 14 May 2020, www.pewresearch.org/social-trends/2020/05/14/

on-the-cusp-of-adulthood-and-facing-an-uncertain-future-what-we-know-about-gen-z-so-far-2/.

85. Garvey, Brian. "Absence of Evidence, Evidence of Absence, and the Atheist's Teapot." Ars Disputandi, vol. 10, no. 1, Jan. 2010, pp. 9–22, https://doi.org/10.1080/15665399.2010.10820011

86. Lincoln, Maya, and Avi Wasser. "Spontaneous Creation of the Universe Ex Nihilo." Physics of the Dark Universe, vol. 2, no. 4, Dec. 2013, pp. 195–99, https://doi.org/10.1016/j.dark.2013.11.004

87. Page, Don N. "The Hartle-Hawking Proposal for the Quantum State of the Universe." The Creation of Ideas in Physics, 1995, pp. 181–87, https://doi.org/10.1007/978-94-011-0037-3_9

88. Staff, Science X. "New String-Theory Notion Redefines the Big Bang." Phys.org, Phys.org, 31 Mar. 2006, https://phys.org/news/2006-03-string-theory-notion-redefines-big.html

89. Steinhardt, Paul J., and Neil Turok. "The Cyclic Model Simplified." New Astronomy Reviews, vol. 49, no. 2-6, May 2005, pp. 43–57, https://doi.org/10.1016/j.newar.2005.01.003

90. Guth, Alan H. "Eternal Inflation and Its Implications." Journal of Physics A: Mathematical and Theoretical, vol. 40, no. 25, June 2007, pp. 6811–26, https://doi.org/10.1088/1751-8113/40/25/s25

91. Guth, Alan H. "Eternal Inflation and Its Implications." Journal of Physics A: Mathematical and Theoretical, vol. 40, no. 25, June 2007, pp. 6811–26, https://doi.org/10.1088/1751-8113/40/25/s25

92. Haerpfer, C., Inglehart, R., Moreno, A., Welzel, C., Kizilova, K., Diez-Medrano J., M. Lagos, P. Norris, E. Ponarin & B. Puranen (eds.). 2022. World Values Survey: Round Seven – Country-Pooled Datafile Version 4.0.0. Madrid, Spain & Vienna, Austria: JD Systems Institute & WVSA Secretariat. doi:10.14281/18241.18

93. Inglehart, R., C. Haerpfer, A. Moreno, C. Welzel, K. Kizilova, J. Diez-Medrano, M. Lagos, P. Norris, E. Ponarin & B. Puranen et al. (eds.). 2018. World Values Survey: Round Six - Country-Pooled Datafile. Madrid, Spain & Vienna, Austria: JD Systems Institute & WVSA Secretariat. doi.org/10.14281/18241.8.

94. Kragh, Helge. "Physics and the Totalitarian Principle." *ArXiv. org*, 2019, https://doi.org/10.48550/arXiv.1907.04623

95. Goyal, Prateek. "How Sadhguru Built His Isha Empire. Illegally." *Newslaundry*, Newslaundry, 17 May 2021, www.newslaundry.com/2021/05/17/how-sadhguru-built-his-isha-empire-illegally

96. Giuffrida, Angela. "Pressure on Italian Catholic Church to Face Child Sexual Abuse Reckoning." *The Guardian*, The Guardian, 11 Feb. 2022, www.theguardian.com/world/2022/feb/11/pressure-on-italy-catholic-church-face-child-sexual-abuse-reckoning

97. "Panini | Indian Grammarian | Britannica." *Encyclopædia Britannica*, 2022, www.britannica.com/biography/Panini-Indian-grammarian

98. "Greek Science." *Oxford Reference*, 2012, www.oxfordreference.com/view/10.1093/acref/9780191736476.timeline.0001.

99. "Inquisition | Definition, History, & Facts | Britannica." Encyclopædia Britannica, 2022, www.britannica.com/topic/inquisition

100. "Miḥnah | Islamic History | Britannica." Encyclopædia Britannica, 2022, www.britannica.com/topic/mihnah

101. Plato. The Republic of Plato. Cambridge University Press, 2009.

102. Chen, Mia. Natural Xenophobia. https://cas.nyu.edu/content/dam/nyu-as/casEWP/documents/w4-2017/chen.pdf

103. "The Truth about Migration: How Evolution Made Us Xenophobes." New Scientist, New Scientist, 6 Apr. 2016, www.newscientist.com/article/mg23030680-800-the-truth-about-migration-how-evolution-made-us-xenophobes

104. "Study Shows Trustworthy People Perceived to Look Similar to Ourselves." ScienceDaily, 2013, www.sciencedaily.com/releases/2013/11/131107094406.htm

105. Buss, David M. "The Evolution of Love in Humans." ResearchGate, unknown, 10 Dec. 2018, www.researchgate.net/publication/329539118_Th_e_Evolution_of_Love_in_Humans

106. "Violence and Climate Change in Prehistoric Egypt and Sudan - British Museum Blog." British Museum Blog - Explore Stories from the Museum, 14 July 2014, https://blog.britishmuseum.org/violence-and-climate-change-in-prehistoric-egypt-and-sudan/

107. Scham, Sandra. "The World's First Temple." Archaeology, vol. 61, no. 6, 2008. Archaeological Institute of America.

108. "Pyramid Texts | Egyptian Religion | Britannica." Encyclopædia Britannica, 2022, www.britannica.com/topic/Pyramid-Texts

109. "Minoan Civilization | History, Location, & Facts | Britannica." Encyclopædia Britannica, 2022, www.britannica.com/topic/Minoan-civilization

110. Jones, Josh. "The Epic of Gilgamesh, the Oldest-Known Work of Literature in World History." Open Culture, 2019, www.openculture.com/2021/07/the-epic-of-gilgamesh-the-oldest-known-work-of-literature-in-world-history.html

111. "Rigveda | Definition & Facts | Britannica." Encyclopædia Britannica, 2022, www.britannica.com/topic/Rigveda

112. "Epic of Gilgamesh | Summary, Characters, & Facts | Britannica." Encyclopædia Britannica, 2022, www.britannica.com/topic/Epic-of-Gilgamesh

113. Burton, Elizabeth. "Akhenaten: The Forgotten Pioneer of Atenism and Monotheism." TheCollector, TheCollector, 9 May 2020, www.thecollector.com/akhenaten-monotheism/

114. Hezariyan, Hojjatollah, and Ghaffar Pourbakhtiar. "A Historical Study of the Persian Gulf and Indo-Arab Trade until the 5th Century AH." Turkish Journal of Computer and Mathematics Education, vol. 12, no. 11, May 2021.

115. "India-China Relations: A Historical and Civilizational Perspective | C3S India | Chennai Centre for China Studies." C3sindia.org, 15 Dec. 2010, www.c3sindia.org/archives/india-china-relations-a-historical-and-civilizational-perspective/

116. "Opium Wars | Definition, Summary, Facts, & Causes | Britannica." Encyclopædia Britannica, 2022, www.britannica.com/topic/Opium-Wars

117. "First Sino-Japanese War | Facts, Definition, History, & Causes | Britannica." Encyclopædia Britannica, 2022, www.britannica.com/event/First-Sino-Japanese-War-1894-1895

118. "Manu-Smriti | Hindu Law | Britannica." Encyclopædia Britannica, 2022, www.britannica.com/topic/Manu-smriti

119. Inter-Caste Marriages in India: Has It Really Changed over Time? https://epc2010.princeton.edu/papers/100157#:~:text=Table%201%20shows%20that%20in

120. Seventh International Conference of American States. Montevideo Convention on the Rights and Duties of States. 1933.

121. "Opinion | Fifteen Years Ago, America Destroyed My Country (Published 2018)." The New York Times, 2022, www.nytimes.com/2018/03/19/opinion/iraq-war-anniversary-.html

122. "Syria's War and the Descent into Horror." Council on Foreign Relations, 2019, www.cfr.org/article/syrias-civil-war

123. The Secretariat of the United Nations. TREATIES DEPOSITED with the SECRETARY-GENERAL close to UNIVERSAL PARTICIPATION. 27 May 2016.

124. Confucius. *Wisdom of Confucius.* S.L., Blurb, 2019.

125. P Lakshmi Narasu. *The Essence of Buddhism.* Literary Licensing, 2014.

126. "Taoism | National Geographic Society." *Nationalgeographic.org*, 2022, education.nationalgeographic.org/resource/taoism.

127. Roy, Nilanjana S. "Homosexuality in India: A Literary History." India Ink, 24 Feb. 2012, archive.nytimes.com/india.blogs.nytimes.com/2012/02/24/homosexuality-in-india-a-literary-history/

128. "Christian Intolerance of Homosexuality on JSTOR." *Jstor.org*, 2022, www.jstor.org/stable/2779118

129. Aziz, Nursyazana. "Homosexuality in Islam." *Academia.edu*, 21 Nov. 2015, www.academia.edu/18780891/Homosexuality_in_Islam

130. Deutsche Welle (www.dw.com. "How George Floyd's Death Reignited a Worldwide Movement | DW | 07.03.2021." *DW.COM*, 2021, www.dw.com/en/how-george-floyds-death-reignited-a-worldwide-movement/a-56781938

131. ET Online. "1998-2022 Salman Khan Blackbuck Poaching Case: A Recap of Events Spanning over Two Decades." The Economic Times. https://economictimes.indiatimes.com/magazines/panache/1998-2022-salman-khan-blackbuck-poaching-case-a-recap-of-events-spanning-over-two-decades/articleshow/90373213.cms

132. "Belgium - Individual - Taxes on Personal Income." Pwc.com, 2022, https://taxsummaries.pwc.com/belgium/individual/taxes-on-personal-income

133. "Sweden - Individual - Taxes on Personal Income." Pwc.com, 2022, https://taxsummaries.pwc.com/sweden/individual/taxes-on-personal-income

134. "Denmark - Individual - Taxes on Personal Income." Pwc.com, 2022, https://taxsummaries.pwc.com/denmark/individual/taxes-on-personal-income

135. "Mongolia - Individual - Taxes on Personal Income." Pwc.com, 2022, https://taxsummaries.pwc.com/mongolia/individual/taxes-on-personal-income

136. "Kazakhstan - Individual - Taxes on Personal Income." Pwc.com, 2021, https://taxsummaries.pwc.com/kazakhstan/individual/taxes-on-personal-income

137. "Taxes in Russia: A Guide to the Russian Tax System." Expat Guide to Russia | Expatica, Expat Guide to Russia | Expatica, 7 Feb. 2022, www.expatica.com/ru/finance/taxes/taxes-in-russia-104125/

138. "Money Matters to Happiness—Perhaps More than Previously Thought | Penn Today." Penn Today, 18 Jan. 2021, https://

penntoday.upenn.edu/news/money-matters-to-happiness-perhaps-more-than-previously-thought

139. Thompson, Helen. "What Does It Really Mean to Be 99 Percent Chimp?" *Smithsonian Magazine*, Smithsonian Magazine, 19 June 2015, www.smithsonianmag.com/smart-news/what-does-being-99-percent-chimp-mean-180955645/

140. Susskind, Daniel. WORLD without WORK : Technology, Automation and How We Should Respond. Penguin Books, 2021.

141. Burrows, Sara. "85% of People Hate Their Jobs, Gallup Poll Says." Return to Now, 22 Sept. 2017, https://returntonow.net/2017/09/22/85-people-hate-jobs-gallup-poll-says/

142. Chugh, Abhinav, and World Economic Forum. "What Is the Great Resignation and What Can We Learn from It." World Economic Forum, 29 Nov. 2021, www.weforum.org/agenda/2021/11/what-is-the-great-resignation-and-what-can-we-learn-from-it/

143. Tesla. "What Is Tesla Full Self-Driving?" J.D. Power, 2022, www.jdpower.com/cars/shopping-guides/what-is-tesla-full-self-driving

144. "Japan Automakers to Fit Cars with Level 2 Self-Driving Tech by 2022." Nikkei Asia, Nikkei Asia, 28 Dec. 2021, https://asia.nikkei.com/Business/Automobiles/Japan-automakers-to-fit-cars-with-level-2-self-driving-tech-by-2022

145. Balmaseda, Liz. "Meet Bionic Bella, Your New Restaurant Waiter: She's Strong, Charming and Moody." The Palm Beach Post, Palm Beach Post, 13 Jan. 2022, www.palmbeachpost.com/story/entertainment/dining/2022/01/13/robot-servers-florida-bellabot-hit-restaurant-customers-boca/9134250002/

146. Spencer, Christian. "Restaurant Hires $1000-a-Month Robot Waiter, Leading to Tip Surge." TheHill, 19 Oct. 2021, https://thehill.com/changing-america/resilience/smart-cities/577452-restaurant-hires-1000-a-month-robot-waiter-and-tips

147. Blue, Sentient. "Sentient Blue Technologies – Enabling Better UAV Flight." Sentientblue.com, 2022, www.sentientblue.com/

148. "Drone Data Solutions for Construction, Volume Estimation & Inspection | Skylark Drones." Skylarkdrones.com, 2022, www.skylarkdrones.com/

149. Keefe, John. "The Present and Potential of AI in Journalism." Knight Foundation, 2021, https://knightfoundation.org/articles/the-present-and-potential-of-ai-in-journalism/

150. Gallego, Jelor. "New Robot Can Operate on Eyes with More Accuracy than a Human Surgeon." Futurism, Futurism, 7 Nov. 2016, https://futurism.com/new-robot-can-operate-on-eyes-with-more-accuracy-than-a-human-surgeon

151. human, Ancient. "Ancient Human Ancestor's Teeth Reveal Diverse Diet." ASU News, 3 June 2013, https://news.asu.edu/content/ancient-human-ancestors-teeth-reveal-diverse-diet

152. "R/Antiwork." Reddit, www.reddit.com/r/antiwork

153. The Economist. "A Study Finds Nearly Half of Jobs Are Vulnerable to Automation." *The Economist*, The Economist, 24 Apr. 2018, www.economist.com/graphic-detail/2018/04/24/a-study-finds-nearly-half-of-jobs-are-vulnerable-to-automation

154. "Signal Messenger: Speak Freely." Signal Messenger, 2013, https://signal.org/en/

155. "Top CEOs Make 300 Times More than Typical Workers: Pay Growth Surpasses Stock Gains and Wage Growth of Top 0.1 Percent." Economic Policy Institute, 2015, www.epi.org/publication/top-ceos-make-300-times-more-than-workers-pay-growth-surpasses-market-gains-and-the-rest-of-the-0-1-percent

156. King, Gilbert. "The Rise and Fall of Nikola Tesla and His Tower." Smithsonian Magazine, Smithsonian Magazine, 4 Feb. 2013, www.smithsonianmag.com/history/the-rise-and-fall-of-nikola-tesla-and-his-tower-11074324

157. "Oscar Wilde | Biography, Books, & Facts | Britannica." Encyclopædia Britannica, 2022, www.britannica.com/biography/Oscar-Wilde

158. PEA. "The Exonian." The Exonian, 21 Mar. 2019, https://theexonian.net/news/2019/03/21/pea-accepts-15-percent-of-applicants

159. "Tuition & Payment Options." Phillips Exeter Academy, 2022, www.exeter.edu/admissions-and-financial-aid/tuition-financial-aid/payment-options

160. Jose Antonio Vargas. "Mark Zuckerberg Opens Up." The New Yorker, The New Yorker, 13 Sept. 2010, www.newyorker.com/magazine/2010/09/20/the-face-of-facebook

161. Locke, Taylor. "How Bill Gates' Mom Helped Microsoft Get a Deal with IBM in 1980 – and It Propelled the Company's Huge Success." CNBC, CNBC, 5 Aug. 2020, www.cnbc.com/2020/08/05/how-bill-gates-mother-influenced-the-success-of-microsoft.html

162. Mejia, Zameena. "Jeff Bezos Got His Parents to Invest Nearly $250,000 in Amazon in 1995 — They Might Be Worth $30 Billion Today." CNBC, CNBC, 2 Aug. 2018, www.cnbc.com/2018/08/02/how-jeff-bezos-got-his-parents-to-invest-in-amazon--turning-them-into.html

163. "Baby Begins to Develop Self-Awareness (15-24 Months) – Parenting Counts." Parentingcounts.org, 2022, www.parentingcounts.org/baby-begins-to-develop-self-awareness-15-24-months/

164. Kanakogi, Yasuhiro, et al. "Preverbal Infants Affirm Third-Party Interventions That Protect Victims from Aggressors." Nature Human Behaviour, vol. 1, no. 2, Jan. 2017, https://doi.org/10.1038/s41562-016-0037

165. "Does Sharing Come Naturally to Kids?" Greater Good, 2022, https://greatergood.berkeley.edu/article/item/does_sharing_come_naturally_to_kids

166. Marx, Karl, and Friedrich Engels. The Communist Manifesto. Vintage Classic, 1848
Fiori, Stefano. "Riassunto." Cahiers d'Economie Politique, vol. 49, no. 2, L'Harmattan, 2022, pp. 19–31,

167. "Does Trickle-down Economics Work?" The Balance, 2021, www.thebalance.com/trickle-down-economics-theory-effect-does-it-work-3305572

168. World Bank Group. "Nearly Half the World Lives on Less than \$5.50 a Day." World Bank, World Bank Group, 17 Oct. 2018, www.worldbank.org/en/news/press-release/2018/10/17/nearly-half-the-world-lives-on-less-than-550-a-day

169. "Alice Walton." Forbes, 2022, www.forbes.com/profile/alice-walton/?sh=5c0fb60d4eb2

170. Trotsky, Leon. Permanent Revolution. 1930. Lightning Source, 2011.

171. FastStats - Deaths and Mortality. 2022, www.cdc.gov/nchs/fastats/deaths.htm

172. "U.S. Wealth Distribution in 2016 | Statista." Statista, Statista, 2016, www.statista.com/statistics/203961/wealth-distribution-for-the-us/

173. Yang, Andrew. "The Freedom Dividend, Defined - Yang2020 - Andrew Yang for President." Yang2020 - Andrew Yang for President, 2020, https://2020.yang2020.com/what-is-freedom-dividend-faq/

174. U.S. Mission Geneva. "U.S. Explanation of Vote on the Right to Food." U.S. Mission to International Organizations in Geneva, 24 Mar. 2017, https://geneva.usmission.gov/2017/03/24/u-s-explanation-of-vote-on-the-right-to-food/

175. "SWZ | the Right to Food around the Globe | Food and Agriculture Organization of the United Nations." Fao.org, 2012, www.fao.org/right-to-food-around-the-globe/countries/swz/en/

176. "SGP | the Right to Food around the Globe | Food and Agriculture Organization of the United Nations." Fao.org, 2013, www.fao.org/right-to-food-around-the-globe/countries/sgp/en/

177. "Children's Right to Education: Where Does the World Stand?" Right to Education Initiative, 2014, www.right-to-education.org/blog/children-s-right-education-where-does-world-stand

178. "How Many People Have Smartphones Worldwide (Mar 2022)." BankMyCell, 10 July 2018, www.bankmycell.com/blog/how-many-phones-are-in-the-world

179. "5 under 25: The Young Entrepreneurs You Should Know." Intelli Bookkeeping, 16 Aug. 2016, https://intellibookkeeping.com/5-25-young-entrepreneurs/

180. Guardian staff reporter. "Smallville Actor Allison Mack Sentenced to Three Years for Role in Nxivm Cult." The Guardian, The Guardian, 30 June 2021, www.theguardian.com/us-news/2021/jun/30/smallville-actor-allison-mack-nxivm-cult

181. Ma, Wayne. "Seven Apple Suppliers Accused of Using Forced Labor from Xinjiang." The Information, The Information, 10 May 2021, www.theinformation.com/articles/seven-apple-suppliers-accused-of-using-forced-labor-from-xinjiang

182. Simina Mistreanu. "Study Links Nike, Adidas and Apple to Forced Uighur Labor." Forbes, 10 Dec. 2021, www.forbes.com/sites/siminamistreanu/2020/03/02/study-links-nike-adidas-and-apple-to-forced-uighur-labor/?sh=2f5ef3631003

183. "Disney World in Which Chinese Children 'Toil for 76 Hours a Week.'" The Independent, 11 Nov. 2010, www.independent.co.uk/news/world/politics/disney-world-in-which-chinese-children-toil-for-76-hours-a-week-2130870.htm

184. Guinnessworldrecords.com, 2022, www.guinnessworldrecords.com/world-records/longest-burning-light-bulb

185. Hadhazy, Adam. "Here's the Truth about the 'Planned Obsolescence' of Tech." Bbc.com, 2019, www.bbc.com/

future/article/20160612-heres-the-truth-about-the-planned-obsolescence-of-tech

186. "Kodak's Downfall Wasn't about Technology." Harvard Business Review, 15 July 2016, https://hbr.org/2016/07/kodaks-downfall-wasnt-about-technology

187. Krajewski, Markus. "The Great Lightbulb Conspiracy." *IEEE Spectrum*, IEEE Spectrum, 24 Sept. 2014, spectrum.ieee.org/the-great-lightbulb-conspiracy

188. BehavioralEconomics.com. "SABE (Society for the Advancement of Behavioral Economics) 2022 (Stateline, NV)." *BehavioralEconomics.com | the BE Hub*, 29 Mar. 2019, www.behavioraleconomics.com/resources/mini-encyclopedia-of-be/homo-economicus

189. "French Revolution | History, Summary, Timeline, Causes, & Facts | Britannica." *Encyclopædia Britannica*, 2022, www.britannica.com/event/French-Revolution

190. "Business Cycle Dating." *NBER*, 2020, www.nber.org/research/business-cycle-dating

191. Gray, Alex. "3 Charts That Explain Global Inequality." *World Economic Forum*, 20 Jan. 2016, www.weforum.org/agenda/2016/01/3-charts-that-explain-global-inequality/

192. "How Hunter-Gatherers Maintained Their Egalitarian Ways." Psychology Today, 2021, www.psychologytoday.com/us/blog/freedom-learn/201105/how-hunter-gatherers-maintained-their-egalitarian-ways

193. Isakhan, Benjamin. "Re-Thinking Middle Eastern Democracy: Lessons from Ancient Mesopotamia." APSA 2006: Proceedings of the 2006 ..., www-cms.newcastle.edu.au, 2011, www.academia.edu/1017043/Re_thinking_Middle_Eastern_democracy_lessons_from_ancient_Mesopotamia

194. Dey, Monidipa. "MATTER of DEMOCRACY: ANCIENT INDIA HAD FUNCTIONING REPUBLICS." *The Daily Guardian*, 20 Mar. 2022, thedailyguardian.com/matter-of-democracy-ancient-india-had-functioning-republics/

195. Academdemus Education. "Pericles of Athens and His Legacy on Democracy and Politics - by Peter Xiao." *Academus Education*, Academus Education, 20 Aug. 2021, www.academuseducation. co.uk/post/pericles-of-athens-and-his-legacy-on-democracy-and-politics

196. Wilson, Emily. "The Secret of Rome's Success." *The Atlantic*, The Atlantic, 17 Nov. 2015, www.theatlantic.com/magazine/archive/2015/12/the-secret-of-romes-success/413143

197. "American Revolution | Causes, Battles, Aftermath, & Facts | Britannica." *Encyclopædia Britannica*, 2022, www.britannica.com/event/American-Revolution

198. "Haitian Revolution | Causes, Summary, & Facts | Britannica." *Encyclopædia Britannica*, 2022, www.britannica.com/topic/Haitian-Revolution

199. Klein, Ira. "VI. British Intervention in the Persian Revolution, 1905–1909." *The Historical Journal*, vol. 15, no. 4, Dec. 1972, pp. 731–52, https://doi.org/10.1017/s0018246x00003526

200. "An Internet History Timeline: From the 1960s to Now." *Jefferson Online*, 22 Nov. 2016, online.jefferson.edu/business/internet-history-timeline/

201. Roser, Max, et al. "Internet." *Our World in Data*, 14 July 2015, ourworldindata.org/internet

202. "The Truth about the Dark Web – IMF F&D." *IMF*, 2019, www.imf.org/en/Publications/fandd/issues/2019/09/the-truth-about-the-dark-web-kumar

203. Zuboff, Shoshana. *The Age of Surveillance Capitalism: The Fight for the Future at the New Frontier of Power.* London, Profile Books, 2019.

204. James, Joshua I. "Legal Protest and Distributed Denial of Service." *ResearchGate*, unknown, 26 Mar. 2013, www.researchgate.net/publication/259497088_Legal_Protest_and_Distributed_Denial_of_Service

205. Daniels, Joe. "Artificial Intelligence to Police the World Wide Web and IP's for Cyber Crimes without Human Intervention." *EIN*

News, EIN Presswire, 15 July 2021, www.einnews.com/pr_news/546352653/artificial-intelligence-to-police-the-world-wide-web-and-ip-s-for-cyber-crimes-without-human-intervention

206. Selvaraj, A. "Game's up for Cyber Criminals as Chennai Cops Turn to AI for Live-Tracking." *The Times of India*, Times Of India, 7 Sept. 2021, timesofindia.indiatimes.com/city/chennai/games-up-for-cyber-criminals-as-chennai-cops-turn-to-ai-for-live-tracking/articleshow/85996574.cms

207. Moussaïd, Mehdi, et al. "Social Influence and the Collective Dynamics of Opinion Formation." *PLoS ONE*, edited by Attila Szolnoki, vol. 8, no. 11, Nov. 2013, p. e78433, https://doi.org/10.1371/journal.pone.0078433

208. Swatman, Rachel. "Video: Japanese Martial Arts Master Attempts Katana World Record." *Guinnessworldrecords.com*, Guinness World Records, 2 Mar. 2017, www.guinnessworldrecords.com/news/2017/3/video-japanese-martial-arts-master-attempts-katana-world-record-464271

209. "Artist with Autism Draws Near-Exact Cityscapes from Memory after Viewing Just Once." *Www.theepochtimes.com*, 8 May 2022, www.theepochtimes.com/artist-with-autism-draws-near-exact-cityscapes-from-memory-after-viewing-just-once_4322905.html

210. "Ultramarathon Man Dean Karnazes on Running to Get through the Pandemic and Being His Best in the Moment - ABC News." *ABC News*, 12 Aug. 2021, www.abc.net.au/news/2021-08-13/dean-karnazes-on-running-through-the-pandemic/100370166

211. StGeorge, Rob. "Slavisa Pajkic - Electric Man (Aka the Battery Man) - Superhuman 46 - Real Life Superhumans." *Real Life Superhumans*, 3 Apr. 2015, sapienplus.com/slavisa-pajkic-electric-man-superhuman-46/

212. Bishop, Robert. "Chaos (Stanford Encyclopedia of Philosophy)." *Stanford.edu*, 2015, plato.stanford.edu/entries/chaos/

213. Pearl, Judea, et al. *Causal Inference in Statistics : A Primer*. Chichester, West Sussex, Wiley, 2016.

214. Arranz, Adolfo, et al. "Assassination of Japan's Former Prime Minister Shinzo Abe." *Reuters*, 19 July 2022, graphics.reuters.com/JAPAN-ABE/ASSASSINATION/zgpomxaygpd/

215. Amos, Owen. "Boris Johnson Resigns: Five Things That Led to the PM's Downfall." *BBC News*, BBC News, 7 July 2022, www.bbc.com/news/uk-politics-62070422

216. Wong, Tessa. "Sri Lanka: President Gotabaya Rajapaksa Flees the Country on Military Jet." *BBC News*, BBC News, 13 July 2022, www.bbc.com/news/world-asia-62132271

217. The. "Ukraine War in Maps: Tracking the Russian Invasion." *BBC News*, BBC News, 8 Aug. 2022, www.bbc.com/news/world-europe-60506682

218. Taylor, Adam. "Map: The World of Coups since 1950." *Washington Post*, The Washington Post, 22 July 2016, www.washingtonpost.com/news/worldviews/wp/2016/07/22/map-the-world-of-coups-since-1950/

219. Riley, Tess. "Just 100 Companies Responsible for 71% of Global Emissions, Study Says." *The Guardian*, The Guardian, 10 July 2017, www.theguardian.com/sustainable-business/2017/jul/10/100-fossil-fuel-companies-investors-responsible-71-global-emissions-cdp-study-climate-change

220. Kono, Daniel Y., and Gabriella R. Montinola. "Foreign Aid and Climate Change Policy: What Can('T) the Data Tell Us?" *WIDER Working Paper*, UNU-WIDER, 2019, https://doi.org/10.35188/unu-wider/2019/649-4

221. "Global Industrial Emissions: Steeling Through?" *Downtoearth.org.in*, 2014, www.downtoearth.org.in/blog/world/global-industrial-emissions-steeling-through--67770

222. Sky. "Climate Change: Seven Technology Solutions That Could Help Solve Crisis." *Sky News*, Sky, 25 Aug. 2020, news.sky.com/story/climate-change-seven-technology-solutions-that-could-help-solve-crisis-12056397

223. Tove Iren S. Gerhardsen. "India, Brazil Tie Biodiversity Negotiations to Doha Development Package - Intellectual Property Watch." *Intellectual Property Watch*, 15 Dec. 2005, www.ip-watch.org/2005/12/15/india-brazil-tie-biodiversity-negotiations-to-doha-development-package/

224. Limb, Lottie. "Death and Deforestation: The Dirty Palm Oil Companies Supplying the EU." *Euronews*, Euronews.com, 8 Oct. 2021, www.euronews.com/green/2021/10/08/nestle-kellogg-s-linked-to-shocking-palm-oil-abuses-in-papua-new-guinea

225. "Hershey Bars, Global Warming and Deforestation: A Sweet New Policy." *The Equation*, 24 Sept. 2014, blog.ucsusa.org/doug-boucher/hershey-bars-global-warming-and-deforestation-a-sweet-new-policy-666

226. "Living Planet Index." *Livingplanetindex.org*, 2020, www.livingplanetindex.org/home/index

227. Nations, United. "A New Era of Conflict and Violence | United Nations." *United Nations*, United Nations, 2016, www.un.org/en/un75/new-era-conflict-and-violence

228. "The Flynn Effect: Has Human Intelligence Reached Its Peak?" *Varsity Online*, Aug. 2022, www.varsity.co.uk/science/22829

229. Vogels, Emily A., et al. "Americans and 'Cancel Culture': Where Some See Calls for Accountability, Others See Censorship, Punishment." *Pew Research Center: Internet, Science & Tech*, Pew Research Center: Internet, Science & Tech, 19 May 2021, www.pewresearch.org/internet/2021/05/19/americans-and-cancel-culture-where-some-see-calls-for-accountability-others-see-censorship-punishment

230. World Migration Report. Geneva: International Organization for Migration, 2020.

231. "Total Fertility Rate 2022." *Worldpopulationreview.com*, 2022, worldpopulationreview.com/country-rankings/total-fertility-rate

232. Nobles, Jenna, et al. "The Effects of Mortality on Fertility: Population Dynamics after a Natural Disaster." Demography, vol. 52, no. 1, Jan. 2015, pp. 15–38, https://doi.org/10.1007/s13524-014-0362-1

233. and, Education. "One University Set-up Every Week, Two Colleges in a Day since 2014: Govt Data." *News18*, News18, 7 Sept. 2021, www.news18.com/news/education-career/one-university-set-up-every-week-two-colleges-in-a-day-since-2014-govt-data-4174166.html

234. "School Enrollment, Tertiary (% Gross) - Botswana | Data." *Worldbank.org*, 2022, data.worldbank.org/indicator/SE.TER.ENRR?locations=BW.

Appendix to Conclusion

Factor determinations for predicting the future as done in the Conclusion chapter based on a complicated Prediction Path Diagram which has been summarised here.

CLIMATE:

DIRECT FACTORS	ORDER-1 SIGN	ORDER-2 FACTORS	ORDER-2 SIGN	FINAL FACTORS
International Order	(+/-)	Economic System	(-)	(-) HIGH
		Domestic Politics	(-)	(+) MID
Pollution	(+)	International Order	(-)	(-) LOW
		Inorganic Technology	(+)	(+) HIGH
		Industrial Resources	(-)	(+) LOW
		Domestic Politics	(+)	(+) MID
		Economic System	(-)	(-) HIGH

DIRECT FACTORS	ORDER-1 SIGN	ORDER-2 FACTORS	ORDER-2 SIGN	FINAL FACTORS
Inorganic Technology	(+)	Economic System	(+/-)	(-) HIGH
		Morality/Law	(+)	(+) MID
		Sustenance Resources	(+)	(0)
		Human Aptitude	(+)	(0)

BIOSPHERE:

DIRECT FACTORS	ORDER-1 SIGN	ORDER-2 FACTORS	ORDER-2 SIGN	FINAL FACTORS
Climate	(-)	International Order	(+/-)	(+) MID
		Pollution	(+)	(+) LOW
		Inorganic Technology	(+)	(+) LOW
Inorganic Technology	(+)	Economic System	(+/-)	(-) HIGH
		Morality/Law	(+)	(+) MID
		Sustenance Resources	(+)	(0)
		Human Aptitude	(+)	(0)
Organic Technology	(+)	Human Aptitude	(+)	(0)
		Morality/Law	(-)	(+) MID
		Economic System	(+/-)	(-) HIGH
		Inorganic Technology	(+)	(+) LOW

DIRECT FACTORS	ORDER-1 SIGN	ORDER-2 FACTORS	ORDER-2 SIGN	FINAL FACTORS
Human Needs	(-)	Sustenance Resources	(+)	(0)
		Organic Technology	(+)	(+) MID
Pollution	(+)	International Order	(-)	(+) MID
		Inorganic Technology	(+)	(+) LOW
		Industrial Resources	(-)	(0)
		Domestic Politics	(+)	(-) LOW
		Economic System	(-)	(-) HIGH
Conflict	(-)	Domestic Politics	(-)	(-) LOW
		Inorganic Technology	(-)	(+) LOW
		Organic Technology	(-)	(+) MID
		Morality/Law	(+)	(+) MID
		International Order	(+)	(+) MID
		Education	(+)	(0)
		Biosphere	(-)	
		Economic System	(+/-)	(-) HIGH

DIRECT FACTORS	ORDER-1 SIGN	ORDER-2 FACTORS	ORDER-2 SIGN	FINAL FACTORS
International Order	(+)	Economic System	(-)	(-) HIGH
		Domestic Politics	(-)	(-) LOW
Domestic Politics	(+/-)	Biosphere	(-)	
		Land	(+)	(0)
		Morality/Law	(+)	(+) MID
		Education	(+)	(0)
		Conflict	(-)	(-) MID
		International Order	(+)	(+) MID
		Economic System	(+)	(-) HIGH
Economic System	(-)	Domestic Politics	(+)	(-) LOW
		Land	(+)	(0)
		Inorganic Technology	(+)	(+) LOW
		Organic Technology	(+)	(+) MID

POLLUTION:

Direct Factors	Order-1 Sign	Order-2 Factors	Order-2 Sign	Final Factors
International Order	(-)	Economic System	(-)	(-) MID
		Domestic Politics	(-)	(+) LOW

Direct Factors	**Order-1 Sign**	**Order-2 Factors**	**Order-2 Sign**	**Final Factors**
Inorganic Technology	(+)	Economic System	(+/-)	(-) MID
		Morality/Law	(+)	(+) LOW
		Sustenance Resources	(+)	(0)
		Human Aptitude	(+)	(0)
Industrial Resources	(-)	Inorganic Technology	(+)	(+) HIGH
Domestic Politics	(+)	Biosphere	(-)	(-) LOW
		Land	(+)	(+) LOW
		Morality/Law	(+)	(+) LOW
		Education	(+)	(0)
		Conflict	(-)	(0)
		International Order	(+)	(-) MID
		Economic System	(+)	(-) MID
Economic System	(-)	Domestic Politics	(+)	(+) LOW
		Land	(+)	(+) LOW
		Inorganic Technology	(+)	(+) HIGH
		Organic Technology	(+)	(0)

MORALITY/LAW:

DIRECT FACTORS	ORDER-1 SIGN	ORDER-2 FACTORS	ORDER-2 SIGN	FINAL FACTORS
Human Needs	(-)	Sustenance Resources	(+)	(0)
		Organic Technology	(+)	(+) LOW
Education	(+)	Morality/Law	(-)	
		Labour	(+)	(0)
		Human Aptitude	(+)	(+) LOW
		Work	(-)	(0)
Land	(-)	Climate	(-)	(0)
		Conflict	(-)	(0)
Human Aptitude	(+)	Organic Technology	(+)	(+) LOW
		Human Needs	(+)	(+) LOW
		Education	(+)	(+) HIGH

POPULATION:

DIRECT FACTORS	ORDER-1 SIGN	ORDER-2 FACTORS	ORDER-2 SIGN	FINAL FACTORS
Education	(-)	Morality/Law	(-)	(-) HIGH
		Labour	(+)	(0)
		Work	(-)	(0)
		Human Aptitude	(+)	(-) MID

DIRECT FACTORS	ORDER-1 SIGN	ORDER-2 FACTORS	ORDER-2 SIGN	FINAL FACTORS
Inorganic Technology	(-)	Economic System	(+/-)	(+) HIGH (-) MID
		Morality/Law	(+)	(-) HIGH
		Sustenance Resources	(+)	(+) LOW
		Human Aptitude	(+)	(-) MID
Organic Technology	(-)	Human Aptitude	(+)	(-) MID
		Morality/Law	(-)	(-) HIGH
		Economic System	(+/-)	(+) HIGH (-) MID
		Inorganic Technology	(+)	(-) HIGH
Human Needs	(+)	Sustenance Resources	(+)	(+) LOW
		Organic Technology	(+)	(-) LOW

EDUCATION:

DIRECT FACTORS	ORDER-1 SIGN	ORDER-2 FACTORS	ORDER-2 SIGN	FINAL FACTORS
Morality/ Law	(-)	Human Needs	(-)	(-) MID
		Education	(+)	
		Land	(-)	(0)
		Human Aptitude	(+)	(+) MID

DIRECT FACTORS	ORDER-1 SIGN	ORDER-2 FACTORS	ORDER-2 SIGN	FINAL FACTORS
Labour	(+)	Domestic Politics	(+)	(0)
		Human Aptitude	(+)	(+) MID
		Economic System	(-)	(-) LOW
		Human Needs	(-)	(-) MID
Work	(-)	Education	(+)	
		Human Aptitude	(+)	(+) MID
		Inorganic Technology	(+/-)	(0)
		Human Needs	(+)	(-) MID
		Labour	(+)	(-) LOW
		Economic System	(-)	(-) LOW
Human Aptitude	(+)	Organic Technology	(+)	(0)
		Human Needs	(+)	(-) MID
		Education	(+)	

WORK:

DIRECT FACTORS	ORDER-1 SIGN	ORDER-2 FACTORS	ORDER-2 SIGN	FINAL FACTORS
Education	(+)	Morality/Law	(-)	(-) LOW
		Labour	(+)	(+) LOW
		Work	(-)	
		Human Aptitude	(+)	(+) MID

DIRECT FACTORS	ORDER-1 SIGN	ORDER-2 FACTORS	ORDER-2 SIGN	FINAL FACTORS
Human Aptitude	(+)	Organic Technology	(+)	(+) LOW
		Human Needs	(+)	(+) LOW
		Education	(+)	(+) MID
Inorganic Technology	(+/-)	Economic System	(+/-)	(-) HIGH
		Morality/Law	(+)	(-) LOW
		Sustenance Resources	(+)	(0)
		Human Aptitude	(+)	(+) MID
Human Needs	(+)	Sustenance Resources	(+)	(0)
		Organic Technology	(+)	(+) LOW
Labour	(+)	Domestic Politics	(+)	(+) LOW
		Human Aptitude	(+)	(+) MID
		Economic System	(-)	(-) HIGH
		Human Needs	(-)	(+) LOW
Economic System	(-)	Domestic Politics	(+)	(+) LOW
		Land	(+)	(0)
		Inorganic Technology	(+)	(-) MID
		Organic Technology	(+)	(+) LOW

INORGANIC TECHNOLOGY:

DIRECT FACTORS	ORDER-1 SIGN	ORDER-2 FACTORS	ORDER-2 SIGN	FINAL FACTORS
Economic System	(+/−)	Domestic Politics	(+)	(0)
		Land	(+)	(0)
		Inorganic Technology	(+)	
		Organic Technology	(+)	(+) LOW
Morality/ Law	(+)	Human Needs	(−)	(0)
		Education	(+)	(+) MID
		Land	(−)	(0)
		Human Aptitude	(+)	(+) HIGH
Sustenance Resources	(+)	Biosphere	(−)	(0)
		Energy Resources	(+)	(0)
		Inorganic Technology	(+)	
		Labour	(+)	(0)
Human Aptitude	(+)	Organic Technology	(+)	(+) LOW
		Human Needs	(+)	(0)
		Education	(+)	(+) MID

ORGANIC TECHNOLOGY:

DIRECT FACTORS	ORDER-1 SIGN	ORDER-2 FACTORS	ORDER-2 SIGN	FINAL FACTORS
Human Aptitude	(+)	Organic Technology	(+)	
		Human Needs	(+)	(+) MID
		Education	(+)	(+) LOW
Morality/ Law	(-)	Human Needs	(-)	(+) MID
		Education	(+)	(+) LOW
		Land	(-)	(+) LOW
		Human Aptitude	(+)	(+) HIGH
Economic System	(+/-)	Domestic Politics	(+)	(0)
		Land	(+)	(+) LOW
		Inorganic Technology	(+)	(0)
		Organic Technology	(+)	

SUSTENANCE RESOURCES:

DIRECT FACTORS	ORDER-1 SIGN	ORDER-2 FACTORS	ORDER-2 SIGN	FINAL FACTORS
Biosphere	(-)	Climate	(-)	(-) LOW
		Pollution	(+)	(0)
		Inorganic Technology	(+)	(+) HIGH

DIRECT FACTORS	ORDER-1 SIGN	ORDER-2 FACTORS	ORDER-2 SIGN	FINAL FACTORS
		Organic Technology	(+)	(+) LOW
		Human Needs	(-)	(-) MID
		Conflict	(-)	(-) LOW
		International Order	(+)	(+) LOW
		Domestic Politics	(+/-)	(+) MID
		Economic System	(-)	(-) MID
Energy Resources	(+)	Organic Technology	(+)	(+) LOW
		Inorganic Technology	(+)	(+) HIGH
		Industrial Resources	(-)	(0)
		Land	(-)	(-) LOW
		Domestic Politics	(+)	(+) MID
Inorganic Technology	(+)	Economic System	(+/-)	(-) MID
		Morality/Law	(+)	(0)
		Sustenance Resources	(+)	
		Human Aptitude	(+)	(0)

DIRECT FACTORS	ORDER-1 SIGN	ORDER-2 FACTORS	ORDER-2 SIGN	FINAL FACTORS
Labour	(+)	Domestic Politics	(+)	(+) MID
		Human Aptitude	(+)	(0)
		Economic System	(-)	(-) MID
		Human Needs	(-)	(-) MID

ENERGY RESOURCES:

DIRECT FACTORS	ORDER-1 SIGN	ORDER-2 FACTORS	ORDER-2 SIGN	FINAL FACTORS
Organic Technology	(+)	Human Aptitude	(+)	(0)
		Morality/Law	(-)	(+) LOW
		Economic System	(+/-)	(+) LOW
		Inorganic Technology	(+)	(+) HIGH
Inorganic Technology	(+)	Economic System	(+/-)	(+) LOW
		Morality/Law	(+)	(+) LOW
		Sustenance Resources	(+)	(0)
		Human Aptitude	(+)	(0)
Industrial Resources	(-)	Inorganic Technology	(+)	(+) HIGH

DIRECT FACTORS	ORDER-1 SIGN	ORDER-2 FACTORS	ORDER-2 SIGN	FINAL FACTORS
Land	(-)	Climate	(-)	(-) MID
		Conflict	(-)	(-) MID
Domestic Politics	(+)	Biosphere	(-)	(0)
		Land	(+)	(-) MID
		Morality/Law	(+)	(+) LOW
		Education	(+)	(0)
		Conflict	(-)	(-) MID
		International Order	(+)	(0)
		Economic System	(+)	(+) LOW

INDUSTRIAL RESOURCES:

DIRECT FACTORS	ORDER-1 SIGN	ORDER-2 FACTORS	ORDER-2 SIGN	FINAL FACTORS
Inorganic Technology	(+)	Human Aptitude	(+)	Inorganic Technology
		Economic System	(+/-)	
		Morality/Law	(+)	
		Sustenance Resources	(+)	

LAND:

DIRECT FACTORS	ORDER-1 SIGN	ORDER-2 FACTORS	ORDER-2 SIGN	FINAL FACTORS
Climate	(-)	International Order	(+/-)	(+) MID
		Pollution	(+)	(+) LOW
		Inorganic Technology	(+)	(0)
Conflict	(-)	Domestic Politics	(-)	(-) HIGH
		Inorganic Technology	(-)	(0)
		Organic Technology	(-)	(0)
		Morality/Law	(+)	(+) MID
		International Order	(+)	(+) MID
		Education	(+)	(+) LOW
		Biosphere	(-)	(-) MID
		Economic System	(+/-)	(-) LOW

LABOUR:

DIRECT FACTORS	ORDER-1 SIGN	ORDER-2 FACTORS	ORDER-2 SIGN	FINAL FACTORS
Domestic Politics	(+)	Biosphere	(-)	(0)
		Land	(+)	(-) LOW
		Morality/Law	(+)	(+) LOW
		Education	(+)	(+) MID
		Conflict	(-)	(0)

DIRECT FACTORS	ORDER-1 SIGN	ORDER-2 FACTORS	ORDER-2 SIGN	FINAL FACTORS
		International Order	(+)	(0)
		Economic System	(+)	(-) MID
Human Aptitude	(+)	Organic Technology	(+)	(+) LOW
		Human Needs	(+)	(-) LOW
		Education	(+)	(+) MID
Economic System	(-)	Domestic Politics	(+)	(+) MID
		Land	(+)	(-) LOW
		Inorganic Technology	(+)	(0)
		Organic Technology	(+)	(+) LOW
Human Needs	(-)	Sustenance Resources	(+)	(-) LOW
		Organic Technology	(+)	(+) LOW

HUMAN NEEDS:

DIRECT FACTORS	ORDER-1 SIGN	ORDER-2 FACTORS	ORDER-2 SIGN	FINAL FACTORS
Sustenance Resources	(+)	Biosphere	(-)	(-) LOW
		Energy Resources	(+)	(+) LOW
		Inorganic Technology	(+)	(+) HIGH
		Labour	(+)	(+) LOW

DIRECT FACTORS	ORDER-1 SIGN	ORDER-2 FACTORS	ORDER-2 SIGN	FINAL FACTORS
Organic Technology	(+)	Human Aptitude	(+)	(+) LOW
		Morality/Law	(-)	(-) LOW
		Economic System	(+/-)	(-) LOW
		Inorganic Technology	(+)	(+) HIGH

HUMAN APTITUDE:

DIRECT FACTORS	ORDER-1 SIGN	ORDER-2 FACTORS	ORDER-2 SIGN	FINAL FACTORS
Organic Technology	(+)	Human Aptitude	(+)	
		Morality/Law	(-)	(-) HIGH
		Economic System	(+/-)	(0)
		Inorganic Technology	(+)	(0)
Human Needs	(+)	Sustenance Resources	(+)	(+) LOW
		Organic Technology	(+)	(+) HIGH
Education	(+)	Morality/Law	(-)	(-) HIGH
		Labour	(+)	(0)
		Work	(-)	(0)
		Human Aptitude	(+)	

CONFLICT:

DIRECT FACTORS	ORDER-1 SIGN	ORDER-2 FACTORS	ORDER-2 SIGN	FINAL FACTORS
Domestic Politics	(-)	Biosphere	(-)	(-) MID
		Land	(+)	(-) HIGH
		Morality/Law	(+)	(-) LOW
		Education	(+)	(+) MID
		Conflict	(-)	
		International Order	(+)	(+) LOW
		Economic System	(+)	(-) HIGH
Inorganic Technology	(-)	Human Aptitude	(+)	(+) MID
		Economic System	(+/-)	(-) HIGH
		Morality/Law	(+)	(-) LOW
		Sustenance Resources	(+)	(-) LOW
Organic Technology	(-)	Human Aptitude	(+)	(+) MID
		Morality/Law	(-)	(-) LOW
		Economic System	(+/-)	(-) HIGH
		Inorganic Technology	(+)	(+) LOW
Morality/Law	(+)	Human Needs	(-)	(-) LOW
		Education	(+)	(+) MID
		Land	(-)	(-) HIGH
		Human Aptitude	(+)	(+) MID
International Order	(+)	Economic System	(-)	(-) HIGH
		Domestic Politics	(-)	(-) HIGH

DIRECT FACTORS	ORDER-1 SIGN	ORDER-2 FACTORS	ORDER-2 SIGN	FINAL FACTORS
Education	(+)	Morality/Law	(-)	(-) LOW
		Labour	(+)	(0)
		Work	(-)	(0)
		Human Aptitude	(+)	(+) MID
Biosphere	(-)	Climate	(-)	(-) LOW
		Pollution	(+)	(-) LOW
		Inorganic Technology	(+)	(+) LOW
		Organic Technology	(+)	(-) LOW
		Human Needs	(-)	(-) LOW
		Conflict	(-)	
		International Order	(+)	(+) LOW
		Domestic Politics	(+/-)	(-) HIGH
		Economic System	(-)	(-) HIGH
Economic System	(+/-)	Domestic Politics	(+)	(-) HIGH
		Land	(+)	(-) HIGH
		Inorganic Technology	(+)	(+) LOW
		Organic Technology	(+)	(-) LOW

ECONOMIC SYSTEM:

DIRECT FACTORS	ORDER-1 SIGN	ORDER-2 FACTORS	ORDER-2 SIGN	FINAL FACTORS
Domestic Politics	(+)	Biosphere	(-)	(0)
		Land	(+)	(+) HIGH
		Morality/Law	(+)	(+) MID
		Education	(+)	(0)
		Conflict	(-)	(-) HIGH
		International Order	(+)	(-) LOW
		Economic System	(+)	
Land	(+)	Climate	(-)	(0)
		Conflict	(-)	(-) HIGH
Inorganic Technology	(+)	Human Aptitude	(+)	(+) LOW
		Economic System	(+/-)	
		Morality/Law	(+)	(+) MID
		Sustenance Resources	(+)	(0)
Organic Technology	(+)	Human Aptitude	(+)	(+) LOW
		Morality/Law	(-)	(+) MID
		Economic System	(+/-)	
		Inorganic Technology	(+)	(+) MID

DOMESTIC POLITICS:

DIRECT FACTORS	ORDER-1 SIGN	ORDER-2 FACTORS	ORDER-2 SIGN	FINAL FACTORS
Biosphere	(-)	Climate	(-)	(-) MID
		Pollution	(+)	(+) LOW
		Inorganic Technology	(+)	(-) LOW
		Organic Technology	(+)	(-) LOW
		Human Needs	(-)	(-) MID
		Conflict	(-)	(-) HIGH
		International Order	(+)	(+) MID
		Domestic Politics	(+/-)	
		Economic System	(-)	(-) HIGH
Land	(+)	Climate	(-)	(-) MID
Morality/Law	(+)	Conflict	(-)	(-) HIGH
		Human Needs	(-)	(-) MID
		Education	(+)	(+) HIGH
		Land	(-)	(-) HIGH
		Human Aptitude	(+)	(+) MID
Education	(+)	Morality/Law	(-)	(+) MID
		Labour	(+)	(0)
		Work	(-)	(0)
		Human Aptitude	(+)	(+) MID

DIRECT FACTORS	ORDER-1 SIGN	ORDER-2 FACTORS	ORDER-2 SIGN	FINAL FACTORS
Conflict	(-)	Domestic Politics	(-)	
		Inorganic Technology	(-)	(-) LOW
		Organic Technology	(-)	(-) LOW
		Morality/Law	(+)	(+) MID
		International Order	(+)	(+) MID
		Education	(+)	(+) HIGH
		Biosphere	(-)	(-) HIGH
		Economic System	(+/-)	(-) HIGH
International Order	(+)	Economic System	(-)	(-) HIGH
		Domestic Politics	(-)	

INTERNATIONAL ORDER:

DIRECT FACTORS	ORDER-1 SIGN	ORDER-2 FACTORS	ORDER-2 SIGN	FINAL FACTORS
Economic System	(-)	Domestic Politics	(+)	(-) MID
		Land	(+)	(-) HIGH
		Inorganic Technology	(+)	(0)
		Organic Technology	(+)	(0)

DIRECT FACTORS	ORDER-1 SIGN	ORDER-2 FACTORS	ORDER-2 SIGN	FINAL FACTORS
Domestic Politics	(-)	Biosphere	(-)	(-) LOW
		Land	(+)	(-) HIGH
		Morality/Law	(+)	(+) LOW
		Education	(+)	(+) LOW
		Conflict	(-)	(-) MID
		International Order	(+)	
		Economic System	(+)	(+) LOW

Acknowledgements

I would like to acknowledge the assistance and support of my mom, dad, and sister without whom you would not be holding this book today. I have to thank my grandparents - Pushpa Dixit, Mrunalini Shendurnikar, and Ramchandra Shendurnikar - for their constant support and encouragement. Furthermore, I would like to express my gratitude to the beta-readers of various chapters of my book – Vagish Srinivasamurthy, Jaydeep Ranade, Ramchandra Shendurnikar, Ada Pai and Aadi Dubey – who were critical to the contents of the book. Finally, I would like to thank my friends (especially the LS group) and well-wishers. If you've finished reading this book. I would like to thank you as well. Without you, this book would have been meaningless. Thank you.

– END –

www.ingramcontent.com/pod-product-compliance
Lightning Source LLC
Chambersburg PA
CBHW051231130726
47988CB00001B/302